بِسْمِ اللَّهِ الرَّحْمَٰنِ الرَّحِيمِ

In the name of Allah, The All-Merciful,
The Kindest towards believers.

Disclaimer

Contact : Admin@islamiclessonsmadeeasy.com.au

Visit us :

- Facebook.com/islamiclessonsmadeeasy
- Youtube.com/islamiclessonsmadeeasy
- Instagram.com/islamic_lessons_me
- Islamiclessonsmadeeasy.com.au
- Ilme.net.au

The pictures used are the property of Islamic Lessons Made Easy. The content and rulings are taken from various leading scholars and are presented in a simplified manner. Therefore, for the exact definition and explanation, please refer to the original sources.

Second edition

Contents

Transliteration 4

Introduction 5

Conditions of *Wuḍūʾ* 8

How to do *Wuḍūʾ* 10

The 5 daily prayers 21

Pre-conditions of prayer 22

How to pray 24

How to pray *Ṣalāt al-Fajr* 27

How to pray *Ṣalāt al-Ẓuhr* 50

How to pray *Ṣalāt al-ʿAṣr* 74

How to pray *Ṣalāt al-Maghrib* 77

How to pray *Ṣalāt al-ʿIshāʾ* 98

What breaks my prayer? 101

Transliteration

ا	a
ب	b
ت	t
ث	th
ج	j
ح	ḥ
خ	kh
د	d
ذ	dh
ر	r
ز	z
س	s
ش	sh
ص	ṣ
ض	ḍ
ط	ṭ
ظ	ẓ
ع	ʿ
غ	gh
ف	f
ق	q
ك	k
ل	l
م	m
ن	n
ه	h
و	w
ي	y
ـَا / ىٰ / آ	ā
ـِي	ī
ـُو	ū

ʾ - Read with a sudden pause of air.

(saw) - Blessings of Allah be upon him and his family.

(n) - Better not to pronounce it. But if you do pronounce it, you do not pronounce the letter after it.

(as) - Peace be upon him/them.

(swt) - Glorious and Exalted Is He.

Introduction

إِنَّ الصَّلَاةَ تَنْهَىٰ عَنِ الْفَحْشَاءِ وَالْمُنكَرِ وَلَذِكْرُ اللَّـهِ أَكْبَر

Verily prayer keeps (one) away from indecency and evil, and certainly the remembrance of Allah is greater. (29:45)

The Holy Prophet (saw) said:

"If there is a stream (of water) at the door of the house of one of you where he washes himself five times a day, will there be any dirt on your body?"

He was answered: "No".

Then he (saw) said:

"Indeed, the example of the prayer is like the example of the flowing stream. Whenever he keeps up prayer, the sins he has committed between two ritual prayers will be vanished."
(*Wasāil al-shīʿah, v.3, p.7*)

Imām al-Ṣādiq (as) said:

"The first thing that will be questioned from a servant is the prayer. Then if the prayer is accepted, his other (good) deeds will be accepted, but if it is rejected his other (good) deeds will not be accepted either."
(*Wasāʾil al-shīʿah, v.3, p.22*)

Some points

1. Prayer helps a person remember Allah
2. Prayer helps a person to reflect about the aim of creation
3. Prayer is a means of washing away sins
4. Prayer is a means of seeking forgiveness and repentance
5. Prayer is a barrier against future sins
6. Prayer strengthens faith and grants piety
7. Prayer removes negligence
8. Prayer breaks one's ego
9. Prayer removes the curtains of pride, self-love and destroys arrogance
10. Prayer is a means of nurturing the purity of our morals
11. Prayer will take one to their spiritual perfection
12. Prayer invites one to the kingdom of the Heavens
13. Prayer can make one as high as the level of angels
14. Prayer gives value and spirit to other deeds
15. Prayer is a collection of sincere intentions, pure sayings and good deeds
16. Prayer strengthens sincerity
17. Prayer strengthens the spirit and discipline of a person

Before Prayer we must do Wuḍū’

Wuḍū’ is an Islamic ritual wash to prepare for prayer and other acts of worship, such as, the rites of the pilgrimage and before touching the Arabic script of the Holy Qurān.

CONDITIONS OF WUḌŪʾ

1. The water must be *ṭāhir* (ritually pure), no traces of impurity, such as blood, etc
2. The water must be *mutlaq* (absolute), not mixed, such as juice
3. You must have permission to use the water
4. The parts of the body which *wuḍūʾ* is performed on must be *ṭāhir*
5. There cannot be any obstacles preventing water reaching the areas of *wuḍūʾ*
6. Using the water must not be harmful
7. Your intention is to seek closeness to Allah
8. The *wuḍūʾ* must be in the correct order and continuous
9. *Wuḍūʾ* must be performed by the person themselves
10. The top of the head and feet must be dry for wiping

CONDITIONS OF WUḌŪʾ

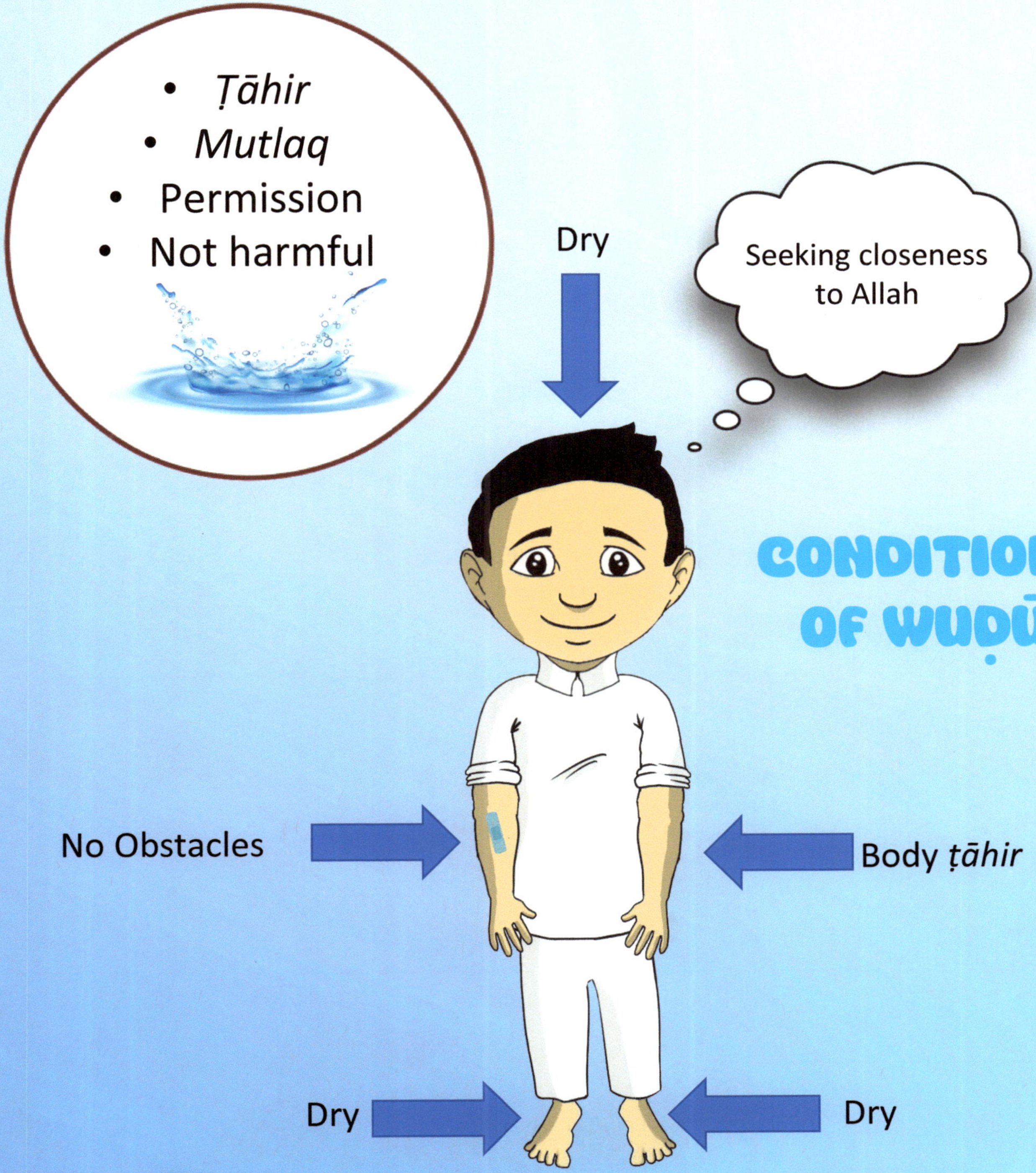

HOW TO DO WUḌŪ'

Niyyah

I am performing
Wuḍū᾿
seeking closeness
to Allah

- First, we make our Intention
- Does not need to be verbal

Mustaḥab

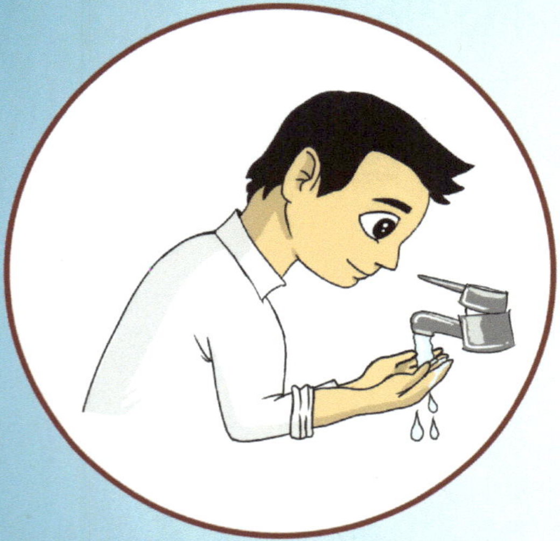

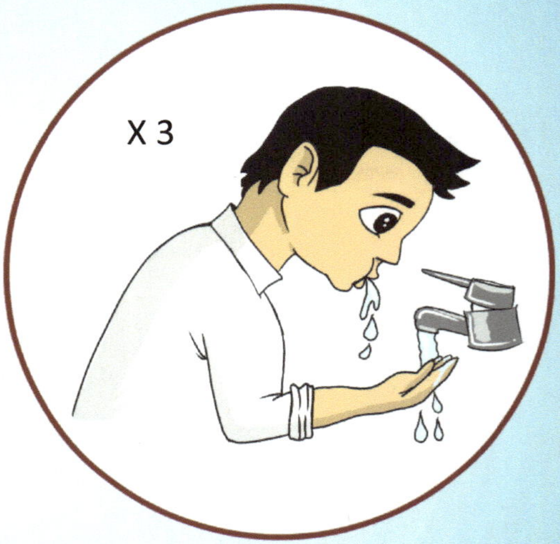

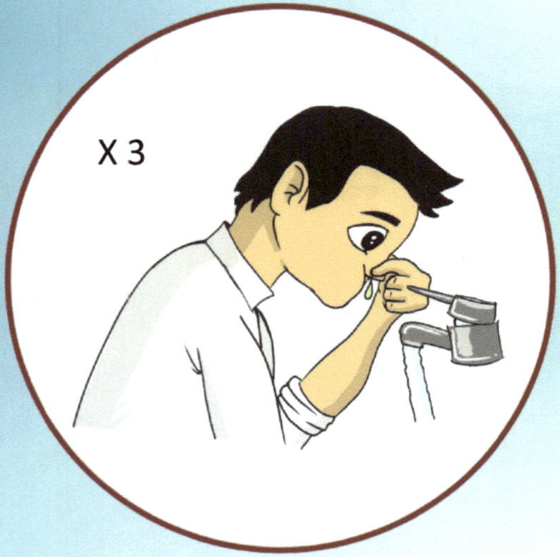

Recommended to

- Wash your hands
- Gargle water in your mouth x 3
- Rinse your nose x 3

Wash Face

Do not wipe in an up and down motion.
Just wipe in a downward direction.

Width – covered by the thumb and middle finger when they are spread out for a normal sized hand

Wash-
Wājib x 1
Mustaḥab x 2
Ḥarām x 3 or more

- Now you must (*Wājib*) wash your face from the top of the forehead where the hair normally grows to the bottom of your chin in a downward direction

- Try to cover the whole face

Wash Arms

Do not wipe in an up and down motion.
Just wipe in a downward direction.

Wash-
Wājib x 1
Mustaḥab x 2
Ḥarām x 3 or more

- Now you first wash your whole right arm starting from the height of the elbow to the fingertips in a downward direction

- Now wash your left arm in the same manner as the right

Wipe Head

Length-
At least the length of one finger

Width –
Wipe with 3 fingers or more

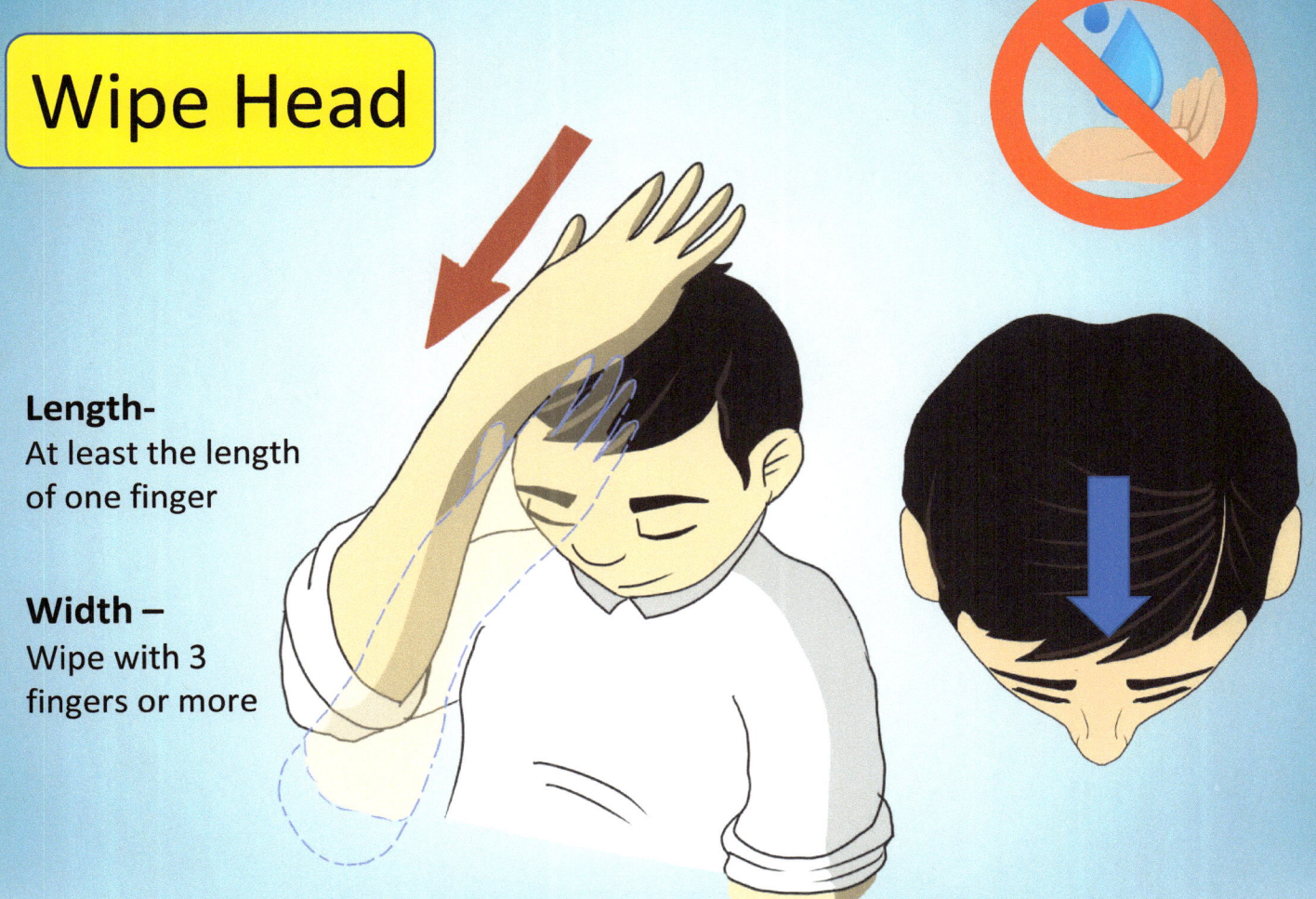

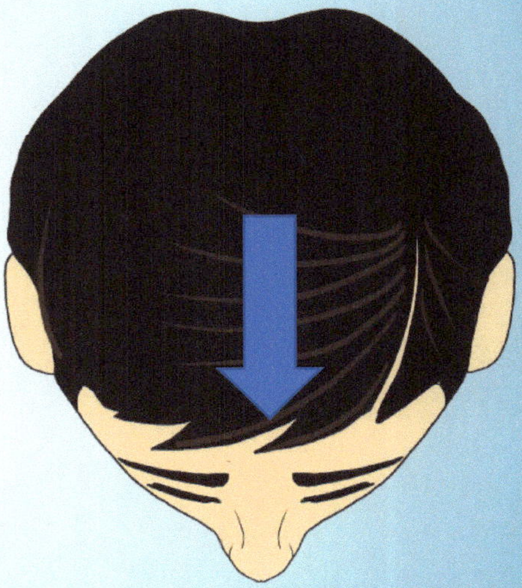

- Now without using any more water, you wipe the front top area of your head with the wetness of water that remained on your right hand

- Recommended precaution to wipe towards the forehead

Wipe Feet

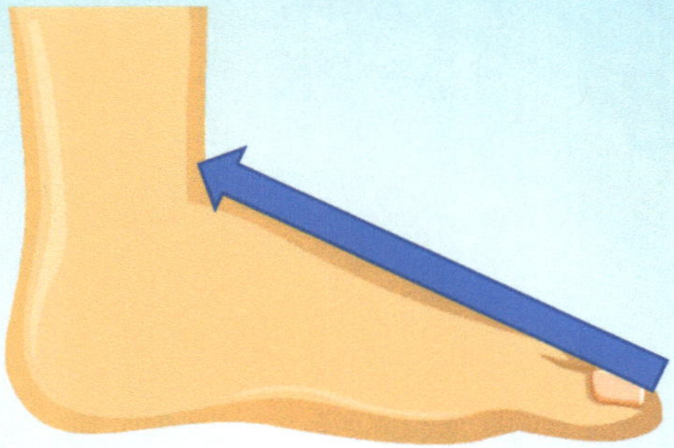

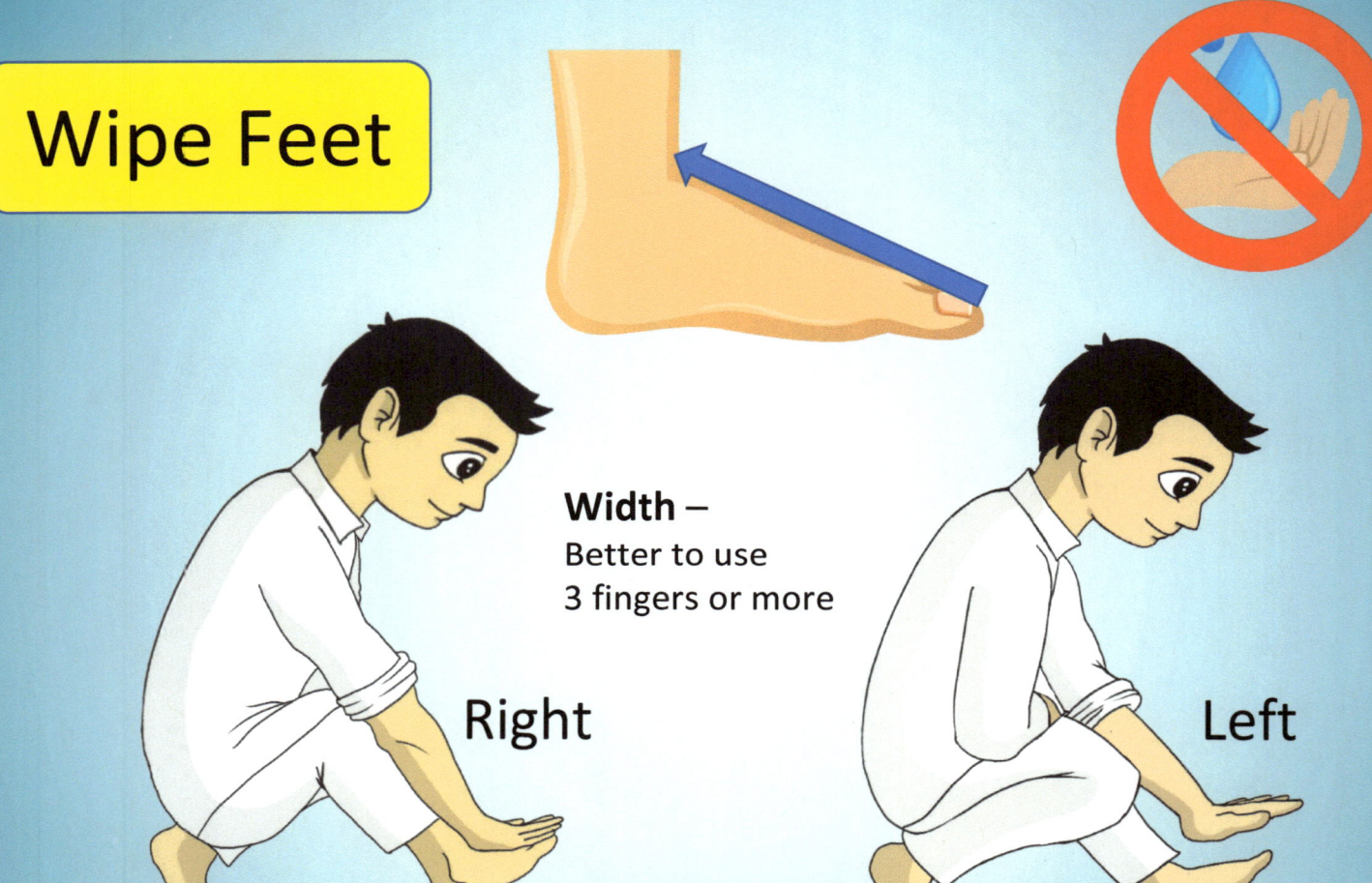

Width –
Better to use
3 fingers or more

Right

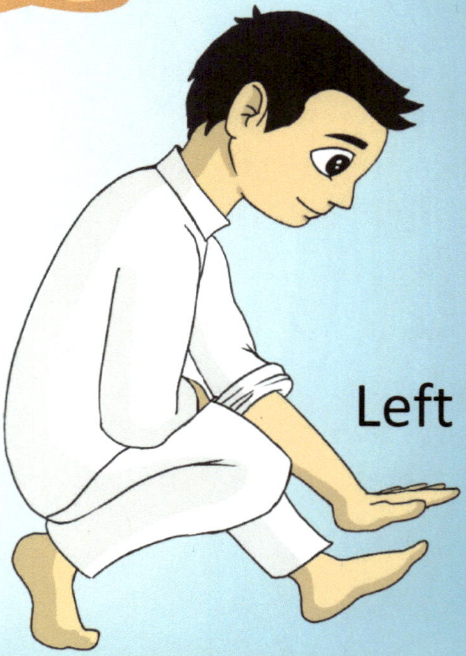

Left

- After wiping the head, using the same wetness, we wipe the feet. The area wiped is from one of the toes to the ankle
- Use the right hand to wipe the right foot first
- Use the left hand to wipe the left foot second

DONE

Now you have completed your *Wuḍūʾ*.
Well done!

For more specifics you can return to our online tutorials or to the original sources

Recommended duas while doing Wuḍū'

When your eyes see the water:
In the name of Allah and by Allah.
All praise is for Allah who made water pure and did not make it impure.

بِسْمِ اللهِ وَبِاللهِ وَالْحَمْدُ للهِ ٱلَّذِي جَعَلَ الْمَآءَ طَهُوراً وَلمْ يَجْعَلْهُ نَجِساً

bismil lāhi wa billāh, wal ḥamdu lillāhil ladhī jaʿalal māʾa ṭahūra(n)w wa lam yajʿalhu najisā

When washing your hands:
In the name of Allah and by Allah.
O Allah! Make me of those who often repent and make me of those who purify themselves.

بِسمِ اللهِ وَبِاللهِ اللّهُمَّ اجعَلْنِي مِنَ التَّوَابِينَ وَاجعَلْنِي مِنَ الْمُتَطَهِّرِينَ

bismil lāhi wa billāh, allāhummajʿalnī minat tawwābīna wajʿalnī minal mutaṭahhirīn

When rinsing your mouth:
O Allah! Instil in me my proof on the day I meet You and make my tongue fluent with Your remembrance.

اللهُمَّ لَقِّنِي حُجَّتِي يَومَ ألقَاكَ وَأطلِقْ لِسَانِي بِذِكرِك

allāhumma laqqinnī ḥujjatī yawma alqāk, wa aṭliq lisānī bidhikrik

When rinsing your nose:
O Allah! Do not deprive me of the fragrance of Paradise, and make me of those who smell its fragrance, its breeze, and its perfume.

اللَّهُمَّ لا تُحَرِّمْ عَلَيَّ رِيحَ الجَنَّةِ،
وَاجعَلنِي مِمَّن يَشُمُّ رِيحَها وَرَوحَها وَطِيبَها

allāhumma lā tuḥarrim ʿalayya rīḥal jannah, wajʿalnī mimma(n)y yashammu rīḥahā wa rawḥahā wa ṭībahā

When washing your face:
O Allah! Brighten my face on the day when [some] faces shall darken, and do not darken my face on the day when [some] faces shall brighten.

اللهُمَّ بَيِّضْ وَجهِي يَومَ تَسوَدُّ فِيهِ الوُجُوهُ،
وَلَا تُسَوِّدْ وَجهِي يَومَ تَبيَضُّ فِيهِ الوُجُوهُ

allāhumma bayyiḍ wajhī yawma taswaddu fīhil wujūh, wa lā tusawwid wajhī yawma tabyaḍḍul fīhil wujūh

Recommended duas while doing Wuḍū'

When washing your right arm:
O Allah! Give me my book [of deeds] in my right hand,
and a permanent stay in Paradise with ease,
and account me [for my deeds] with an easy accounting.

اللّهُمَّ أعطِني كِتابي بيَميني،
والخُلْدَ في الجِنانِ بِيساري، وحاسِبْني حِساباً يَسيراً

allāhumma aʿṭinī kitābī biyamīnī, wal khulda fil jināni biyasārī, wa ḥāsibnī ḥisābay yasīrā

When washing your left arm:
O Allah! Do not give me my book [of deeds]
in my left hand, nor from behind my back,
and do not chain it to my neck. I seek refuge with
You from the garments made from Hell-fire.

اللّهُمَّ لا تُعطِني كِتابي بِشِمالي وَلا مِن وَراءِ ظَهري،
ولا تجعَلْها مَغلُولَةً إلى عُنُقي، وأعُوذُ بِكَ مِن مُقَطَّعَاتِ النِّيرانِ

allāhumma lā tuʿṭinī kitābī bishimālī, wa lā mi(n)w warāʾi ẓahrī, wa lā tajʿalhā maghlūlatan ilā ʿunuqī, wa aʿūdhu bika mi(n)m muqaṭṭaʿātin nīrān

When wiping your head:
O Allah! Surround me in Your mercy,
Your blessings, and Your pardon.

اَللّٰهُمَّ غَشِّنِي بِرَحْمَتِكَ وَ بَرَكَاتِكَ وَ عَفْوِكَ

allāhumma ghashshinī birahmatika wa barakātika wa ʿafwik

When wiping your feet:
O Allah! Keep me firmly on the path on the day when
feet shall stumble, and let my efforts be in those
things that make You pleased with me,
O Possessor of Majesty and Bounty!

اَللّٰهُمَّ ثَبِّتْنِيْ عَلَى الصِّرَاطِ يَوْمَ تَزِلُّ فِيْهِ الْأَقْدَامُ، وَاجْعَلْ
سَعْيِيْ فِيْمَا يُرْضِيْكَ عَنِّيْ يَا ذَا الْجَلَالِ وَالْإِكْرَامِ

allāhumma thabbitnī ʿalaṣ ṣirāti yawma tazillu fīhil aqdām, waj ʿal saʿyī fīmā yurḍīka ʿannī, yā dhal jalāli wal ikrām

WHAT BREAKS MY WUḌŪ'

Using the Toilet

Passing Wind

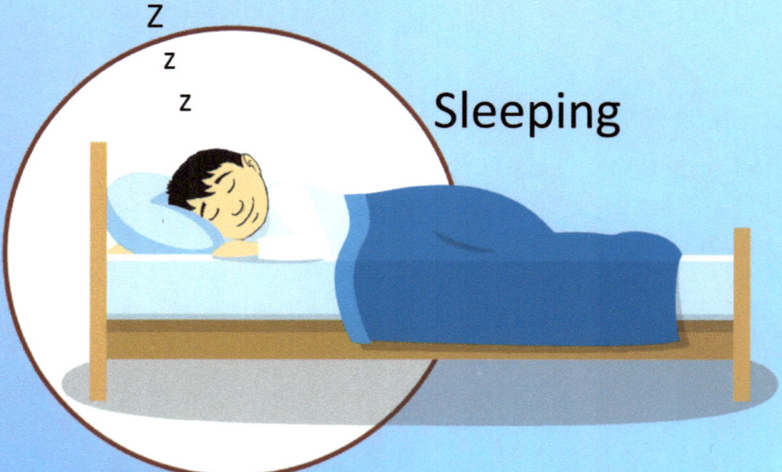

Sleeping

For more specifics you can return to our online tutorials or to the original sources

The 5 Daily Prayers

1 *rakʿah* = 1 x *rukūʿ* and 2 x *sajdahs*

There are 5 *wājib* (obligatory) prayers

Prayer	*Rakʿahs*	Time
Fajr	**2**	From True Dawn until Sunrise
Ẓuhr	**4**	Midday until enough time for the *ʿAṣr* prayer, just before Sunset
ʿAṣr	**4**	After *Ẓuhr* until Sunset
Maghrib	**3**	After Sunset until enough time for the *ʿIshāʾ* prayer before midnight
ʿIshāʾ	**4**	After (*Maghrib*) until midnight

PRE-CONDITIONS OF PRAYER

1. You must pray towards the Holy *Kaʿbah*
2. *Wuḍūʾ* must be performed before prayer
3. Your intention is to seek closeness to Allah
4. You must have permission to use the area you are praying in
5. You only pray a *wājib* prayer when its time comes
6. Your clothes and body must be *ṭāhir* (ritually pure)
7. Your clothes must not be stolen or taken without permission
8. Men cannot wear gold or pure silk
9. Women must cover their entire body except for their face and hands
10. Place of *sajdah* must be *ṭāhir*
11. Covering the feet up to the ankles is not *wājib* for women if there is no non-*maḥram* present

Maḥram means a person who is *ḥarām* for one to marry and/or it is permissible for one to see them without hijab.

There are three categories of *Maḥrams*:

- *Blood-Maḥram,* like aunts and uncles, etc.
- *Maḥram* by marriage, like spouse, mother-in-law, father-in-law, etc.
- *Maḥram* through breast feeding

Therefore, a *non-Maḥram* will be those not in these categories.

PRE-CONDITIONS OF PRAYER

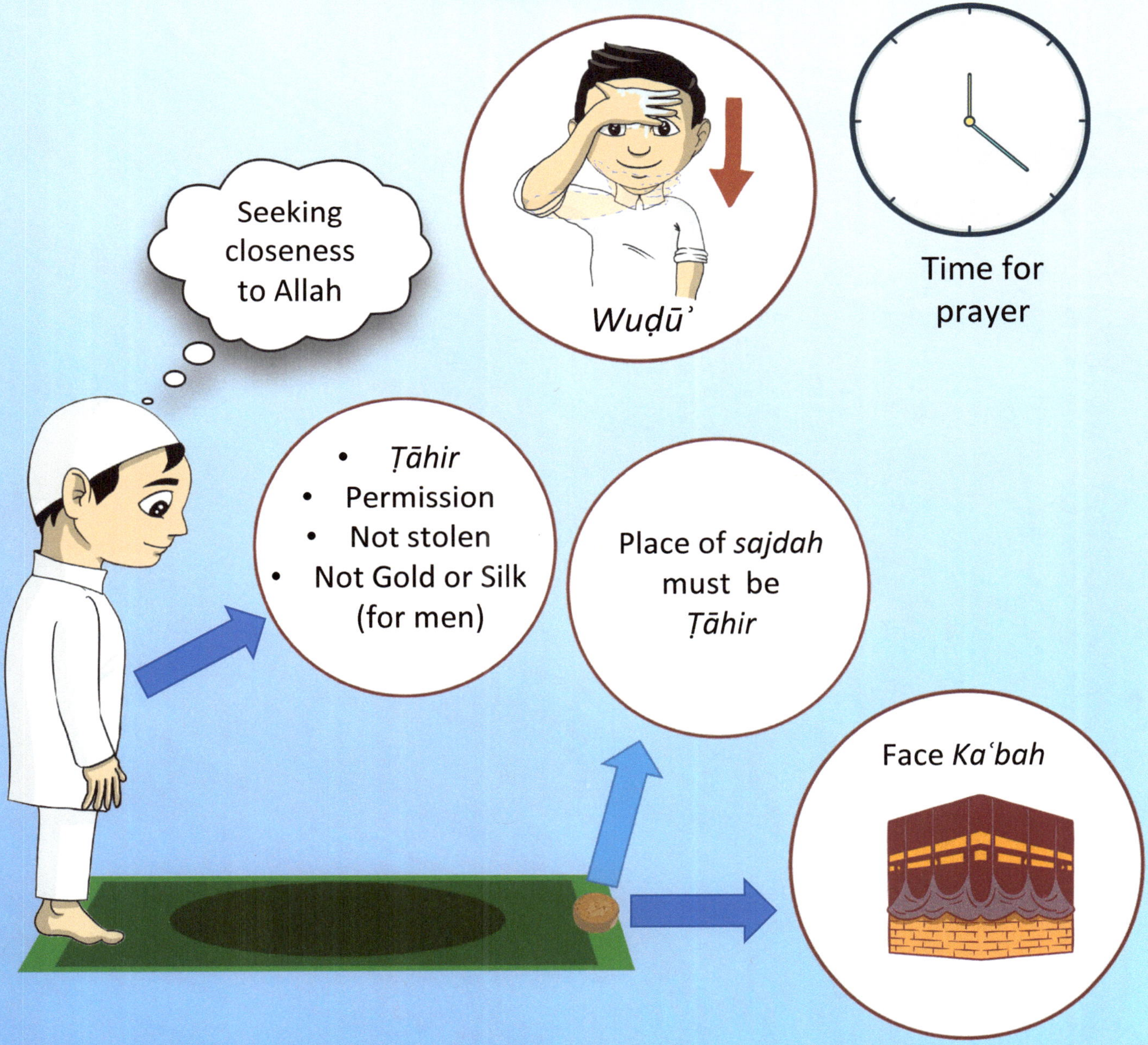

HOW TO PRAY

اللهُ أَكبَر

Allahu Akbar x 4

Allah is greater (than what He is described as)

أَشْهَدُ أَن لا إلَهَ إِلّا الله

Ashhadu a(n)l lā ilāha illal lāh x 2

I testify that there is no god but Allah

أَشهَدُ أَنَّ مُحَمَّداً رَسُولُ الله

Ashhadu anna Muḥammadan rasūlul lāh x 2

I testify that Muḥammad is the messenger of Allah

أَشهَدُ أَنَّ عَلِياً وَلِىُّ الله

Ashhadu anna ʿAliyya(n)w waliyyul lāh x 2

(Not part of *adhān*, but good to say)

I testify that Ali is the appointed guardian of Allah

حَيَّ عَلَى الصَلاة

Ḥayya ʿalaṣ ṣalāh x 2

Hasten to prayer

حَيَّ عَلى الفَلاح

Ḥayya ʿalal falāḥ x 2

Hasten to success

حَيَّ عَلى خَيرِ العَمَل

Ḥayya ʿalā khayril ʿamal x 2

Hasten to the best act

اللهُ أَكبَر

Allahu Akbar x 2

Allah is greater (than what He is described as)

لاَ إِلَهَ إِلّا الله

Lā ilāha illah lāh x 2

There is no god but Allah

- Recommended to say *adhān* and *iqāmah* before the daily prayers in correct Arabic
- Recite when the time of Prayer has set in

Adhān

First call to prayer

- Recommended to say *adhān* and *iqāmah* before the daily prayers in correct Arabic
- Recite when the time of Prayer has set in

Iqāmah

Second call to prayer

الله أكبر
Allahu Akbar x 2
Allah is greater (than what He is described as)

أَشهَدُ أَن لَا إِلَهَ إِلّا الله
Ashhadu a(n)l lā ilāha illal lāh x 2
I testify that there is no god but Allah

أَشهَدُ أَنَّ مُحَمَّداً رَسُولُ الله
Ashhadu anna Muḥammadan rasūlul lāh x 2
I testify that Muḥammad is the messenger of Allah

أَشهَدُ أَنَّ علياً وَلِيُّ الله
Ashhadu anna ʿAliyya(n)w waliyyul lāh x 2
(Not part of *iqāmah*, but good to say)
I testify that Ali is the appointed guardian of Allah

حَيَّ عَلَى الصَلاة
Ḥayya ʿalaṣ ṣalāh x 2
Hasten to prayer

حَيَّ عَلَى الفَلاح
Ḥayya ʿalal falāḥ x 2
Hasten to success

حَيَّ عَلَى خَيرِ العَمَل
Ḥayya ʿalā khayril ʿamal x 2
Hasten to the best act

قَد قَامَتِ الصَلاة
Qad qāmatiṣ ṣalāh x 2
Certainly, the prayer has been established

اللهُ أَكبَر
Allahu Akbar x 2
Allah is greater (than what He is described as)

لا إِلَهَ إِلّا الله
Lā ilāha illah lāh x 1
There is no god but Allah

HOW TO PRAY ṢALĀT AL – FAJR

2 x *rakʿahs*

- Focus on what you are doing
- Focus on who you are standing in front of
- Block out distractions
- Put your heart and mind into prayer
- Face the Kaʿbah
- Stand up straight

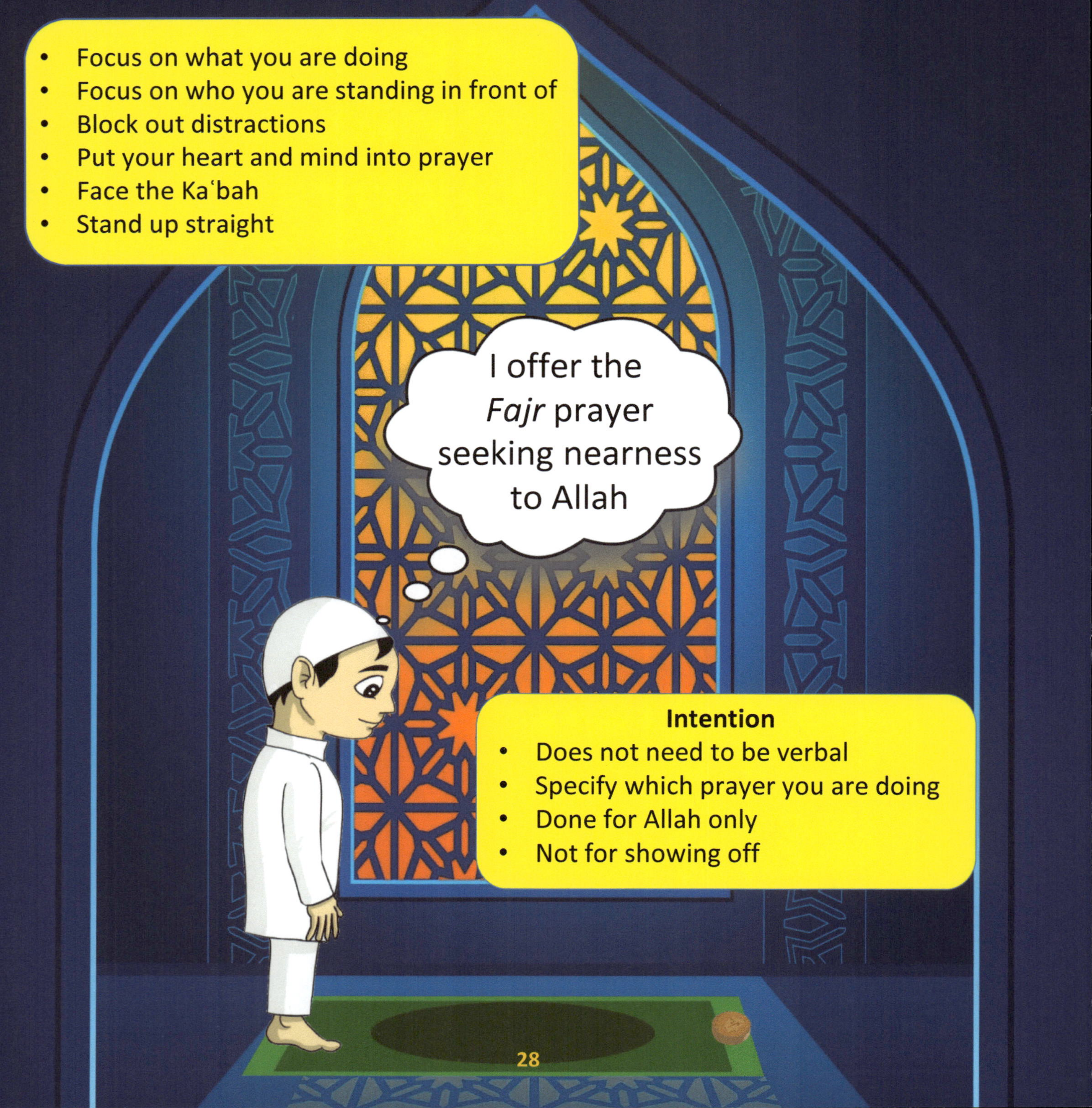
I offer the *Fajr* prayer seeking nearness to Allah

Intention

- Does not need to be verbal
- Specify which prayer you are doing
- Done for Allah only
- Not for showing off

Lift both hands up to your ears and say *Allahu Akbar*
(Allah is greater than what He is described as)

Allahu Akbar

- *Wājib* to say at the beginning of every prayer
- Must be pronounced in correct Arabic
- Body must be still
- Recommended to raise hands to ears

1st *rakʿah*

- Remain standing
- Recite Sūrah al-Fātiḥah
- Recite in clear Arabic
- Males recite aloud
- Females recite aloud or soft, but recite soft in front of a *non-maḥram*

بِسْمِ اللَّـهِ الرَّحْمَـٰنِ الرَّحِيمِ

Bismil lāhir Raḥmānir Raḥīm

I start in the name of Allah, the All Merciful towards all existents, The Kindest towards believers

الْحَمْدُ لِلَّـهِ رَبِّ الْعَالَمِينَ

Alḥamdu lillāhi Rabbil ʿālamīn

All praise and thanks are (just) for Allah, The Nurturer of all worlds

الرَّحْمَـٰنِ الرَّحِيمِ

Arraḥmānir Raḥīm

The All Merciful towards all existents, The Kindest towards believers

مَالِكِ يَوْمِ الدِّينِ

Māliki yawmid dīn

The (only real) Owner of everything (and the only authority) on Judgement day

إِيَّاكَ نَعْبُدُ وَإِيَّاكَ نَسْتَعِينُ

Iyyāka naʿbudu wa iyyāka nastaʿīn

((O Allah!)) You (and only You) we worship and You (and only You) we seek help from (as the independent deity)

اهْدِنَا الصِّرَاطَ الْمُسْتَقِيمَ

Ihdinaṣ ṣirāṭal mustaqīm

Guide (and take) us to the right Path

صِرَاطَ الَّذِينَ أَنْعَمْتَ عَلَيْهِمْ
غَيْرِ الْمَغْضُوبِ عَلَيْهِمْ وَلَا الضَّالِّينَ

Ṣirāṭal ladhīna anʿamta ʿalayhim ghayril maghḍūbi ʿalayhim wa laḍ ḍāllīn

The path of those whom You have bestowed your Blessings upon. Not of those who have earned Your wrath and not (of) those who have gone astray

- Remain standing
- Recite in clear Arabic
- Recite another *Sūrah*
- Males recite aloud
- Females recite aloud or soft, but recite soft in front of a *non-maḥram*

بِسْمِ اللَّـهِ الرَّحْمَـٰنِ الرَّحِيمِ

Bismil lāhir Raḥmānir Raḥīm

I start in the name of Allah, the All Merciful towards all existents, The Kindest towards believers

قُلْ هُوَ اللَّـهُ أَحَدٌ

Qul Huwal lāhu aḥad

Say, He is Allah, the One

اللَّـهُ الصَّمَدُ

Allahuṣ Ṣamad

Allah is Who is independent of all beings

لَمْ يَلِدْ وَلَمْ يُولَدْ

Lam Yalid Wa Lam Yūlad

He has never had an offspring, nor was He born

وَلَمْ يَكُن لَّهُ كُفُوًا أَحَدٌ

Wa Lam Yaku*(n)*l lahu kufuwan aḥad

Nor has He any equal

Lift both hands up to your ears
and say *Allahu Akbar*
(Allah is greater than what He is described as)

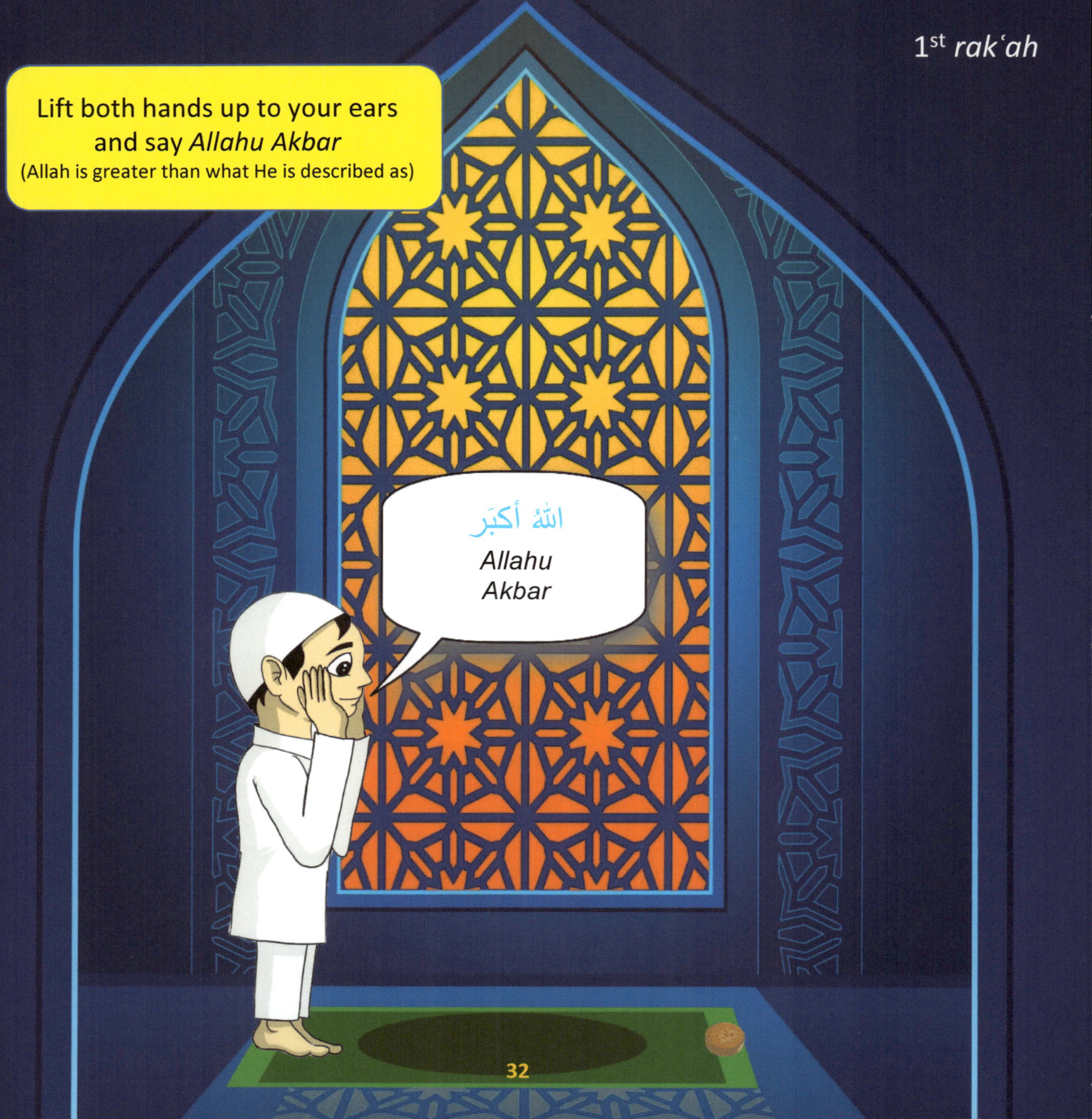

1st *rakʿah*

Rukūʿ

Bowing

- Bend forward and place hands on your knees
- Recite in correct Arabic
- Remain steady
- While in this position recite a *dhikr* (glorification)
- Also recommended to say:

اللّٰهُمّ صَلّ عَلَى مُحَمّدٍ وَآلِ مُحَمّدٍ

Allahumma Ṣalli ʿalā Muḥammadi(n)w wa āli Muḥammad

(O Allah, Bless Muḥammad and the progeny of Muḥammad)

Dhikr

سُبْحانَ رَبِّيَ ٱلْعَظِيمِ وَ بِحَمدِهِ

Subḥāna Rabbiyal ʿaẓīmi wa biḥamdih

I absolutely declare that my Great Nurturer is free from imperfections, and I do so by praising Him

- Stand up straight and still
- Recommended to say *Samiʿal lāhu liman ḥamidah*
  (Allah hears the one who praises Him)
- Then say *Allahu Akbar*
  (Allah is greater than what He is described as)

سَمِعَ اللهُ لِمَن حَمدَه
Samiʿal lāhu liman ḥamidah

الله أكبر
Allahu Akbar

1st *rakʿah*

Sujūd

Prostrating

- Place your forehead on the ground in humility
- Place both palms of your hands, both knees and both big toes on the ground
- Remain still
- Recommended for women to place their elbows on the ground
- Recite in correct Arabic
- While in this position recite a *dhikr* (glorification)
- Also recommended to say:

اللّهُمّ صَلّ عَلَى مُحَمّدٍ وَآلِ مُحَمّدٍ

Allahumma Ṣalli ʿalā Muḥammadi(n)w wa āli Muḥammad

(O Allah, Bless Muḥammad and the progeny of Muḥammad)

You must perform *sajdah* on earth and of those things that grow from the earth but neither edible nor worn, such as wood or leaves. The best thing to perform *sajdah* on is the soil of Imam Hussein (as).

Dhikr

سُبْحانَ رَبِّيَ ٱلأَعْلَىٰ وَ بِحَمدِهِ

Subḥāna Rabbiyal aʿlā wa biḥamdih

I absolutely declare that my Most High Nurturer is free from imperfections, and I do so by praising Him

1st *sajdah*

- After the 1st *sajdah*, it is recommended to sit with the top part of the right foot on the sole of the left foot
- Recommended to place hands on thighs
- Recommended to say *Allahu Akbar*
- Recommended to also say:

اَستَغفِرُ اللهَ رَبِّي وَاتُوبُ اِلَيه

Astaghfirul lāha rabbī wa atūbu ilayh

(I seek forgiveness from Allah, My Nurturer, and I turn to Him in repentance)

1st *rakʿah*

Sujūd

Prostrating

- Place your forehead on the ground in humility
- Perform the 2nd *sajdah* in the same manner as the first

Dhikr

سُبْحَانَ رَبِّيَ ٱلأَعْلَىٰ وَ بِحَمدِهِ

Subḥāna Rabbiyal aʿlā wa biḥamdih

I absolutely declare that my Most High Nurturer is free from imperfections, and I do so by praising Him

2nd *sajdah*

- After the 2nd *sajdah*, sit in the recommended position
- Keep body still
- Recommended to say *Allahu Akbar*

اللهُ أَكبَر
Allahu Akbar

- Stand back up
- While getting up it is recommended to say:
  Biḥawlil lāhi wa quwwatihi aqūmu wa aqʻud
  (I stand and sit by the strength of Allah and by His power)

بِحَوْلِ اللَّهِ وَ قُوَّتِهِ أَقُومُ وَ أَقْعُدُ

Biḥawlil lāhi wa quwwatihi aqūmu wa aqʻud

- Remain standing
- Recite Sūrah al-Fātiḥah
- Recite in clear Arabic
- Males recite aloud
- Females recite aloud or soft, but recite soft in front of a *non-maḥram*

بِسْمِ اللَّـهِ الرَّحْمَـٰنِ الرَّحِيمِ

Bismil lāhir Raḥmānir Raḥīm

I start in the name of Allah, the All Merciful towards all existents, The Kindest towards believers

الْحَمْدُ لِلَّـهِ رَبِّ الْعَالَمِينَ

Alḥamdu lillāhi Rabbil ʿālamīn

All praise and thanks are (just) for Allah, The Nurturer of all worlds

الرَّحْمَـٰنِ الرَّحِيمِ

Arraḥmānir Raḥīm

The All Merciful towards all existents, The Kindest towards believers

مَالِكِ يَوْمِ الدِّينِ

Māliki yawmid dīn

The (only real) Owner of everything (and the only authority) on Judgement day

إِيَّاكَ نَعْبُدُ وَإِيَّاكَ نَسْتَعِينُ

Iyyāka naʿbudu wa iyyāka nastaʿīn

((O Allah!)) You (and only You) we worship and You (and only You) we seek help from (as the independent deity)

اهْدِنَا الصِّرَاطَ الْمُسْتَقِيمَ

Ihdinaṣ ṣirāṭal mustaqīm

Guide (and take) us to the right Path

صِرَاطَ الَّذِينَ أَنْعَمْتَ عَلَيْهِمْ
غَيْرِ الْمَغْضُوبِ عَلَيْهِمْ وَلَا الضَّالِّينَ

Ṣirāṭal ladhīna anʿamta ʿalayhim ghayril maghḍūbi ʿalayhim wa laḍ ḍāllīn

The path of those whom You have bestowed your Blessings upon. Not of those who have earned Your wrath and not (of) those who have gone astray

- Remain standing
- Recite in clear Arabic
- Recite another *Sūrah*
- Males recite aloud
- Females recite aloud or soft, but recite soft in front of a *non-maḥram*

بِسْمِ اللَّـهِ الرَّحْمَـٰنِ الرَّحِيمِ

Bismil lāhir Raḥmānir Raḥīm

I start in the name of Allah, the All Merciful towards all existents, The Kindest towards believers

قُلْ هُوَ اللَّـهُ أَحَدٌ

Qul Huwal lāhu aḥad

Say, He is Allah, the One

اللَّـهُ الصَّمَدُ

Allahuṣ Ṣamad

Allah is Who is independent of all beings

لَمْ يَلِدْ وَلَمْ يُولَدْ

Lam Yalid Wa Lam Yūlad

He has never had an offspring, nor was He born

وَلَمْ يَكُن لَّهُ كُفُوًا أَحَدٌ

Wa Lam Yaku(n)l lahu kufuwan aḥad

Nor has He any equal

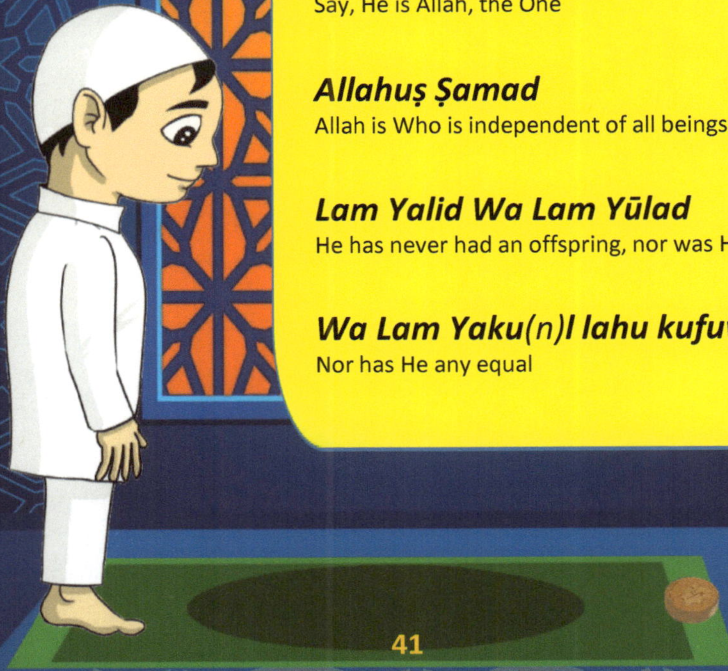

- It is recommended to perform *qunūt* before *rukūʿ* in 2nd *rakʿah*
- Place hands in front of your face with palms facing the sky and both hands and fingers next to each other
- You can say any *dhikr*
- After *dhikr* say *Allahu Akbar*

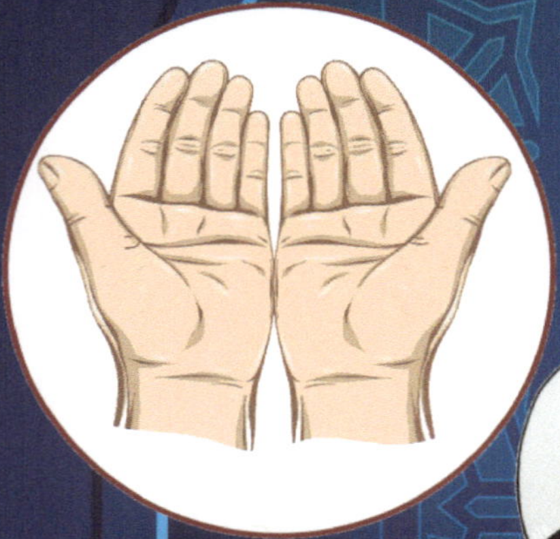

Dhikr

رَبَّنَا أَفْرِغْ عَلَيْنَا صَبْرًا

Rabbanā afrigh ʿalaynā ṣabrā,

Our Nurturer! Shower us with patience,

وَثَبِّتْ أَقْدَامَنَا

wa thabbit aqdāmanā,

And make us stand firm,

وَانصُرْنَا عَلَى الْقَوْمِ الْكَافِرِينَ

wan ṣurnā ʿalal qawmil kāfirīn

And help us against the coverers of the truth

2nd *rakʿah*

Rukūʿ

Bowing

- Bend forward and place hands on your knees
- Recite in correct Arabic
- Remain steady
- While in this position recite a *dhikr* (glorification)
- Also recommended to say:

اللّٰهُمَّ صَلِّ عَلَى مُحَمَّدٍ وَآلِ مُحَمَّدٍ

Allahumma Ṣalli ʿalā Muḥammadi(n)w wa āli Muḥammad

(O Allah, Bless Muḥammad and the progeny of Muḥammad)

Dhikr

سُبْحانَ رَبِّيَ ٱلْعَظيمِ وَ بِحَمدِهِ

Subḥāna Rabbiyal ʿaẓīmi wa biḥamdih

I absolutely declare that my Great Nurturer is free from imperfections, and I do so by praising Him

- Stand up straight and still
- Recommended to say *Samiʿal lāhu liman ḥamidah*
  (Allah hears the one who praises Him)
- Then say *Allahu Akbar*
  (Allah is greater than what He is described as)

سَمِعَ اللهُ لِمَن حَمدَه
Samiʿal lāhu liman ḥamidah

الله أكبر
Allahu Akbar

- Place your forehead on the ground in humility
- Place both palms of your hands, both knees and both big toes on the ground
- Remain still
- Recommended for women to place their elbows on the ground
- Recite in correct Arabic
- While in this position recite a *dhikr* (glorification)
- Also recommended to say:

اللّٰهُمَّ صَلِّ عَلَى مُحَمَّدٍ وَآلِ مُحَمَّدٍ

Allahumma Ṣalli ʿalā Muḥammadi(n)w wa āli Muḥammad

(O Allah, Bless Muḥammad and the progeny of Muḥammad)

Dhikr

سُبْحانَ رَبِّيَ ٱلأَعْلَىٰ وَ بِحَمدِهِ

Subḥāna Rabbiyal aʿlā wa biḥamdih

I absolutely declare that my Most High Nurturer is free from imperfections, and I do so by praising Him

1st *sajdah*

- After the 1st *sajdah*, it is recommended to sit with the top part of the right foot on the sole of the left foot
- Recommended to place hands on thighs
- Recommended to say *Allahu Akbar*
- Recommended to also say :

اَستَغفِرُ اللهَ رَبِّي وَاتُوبُ اِلَيه

Astaghfirul lāha rabbī wa atūbu ilayh

(I seek forgiveness from Allah, My Nurturer, and I turn to Him in repentance)

2nd *rakʿah*

- Place your forehead on the ground in humility
- Perform the 2nd *sajdah* in the same manner as the first

Dhikr

سُبْحانَ رَبِّيَ ٱلاَعْلىٰ وَ بِحَمدِهِ

Subḥāna Rabbiyal aʿlā wa biḥamdih

I absolutely declare that my Most High Nurturer is free from imperfections, and I do so by praising Him

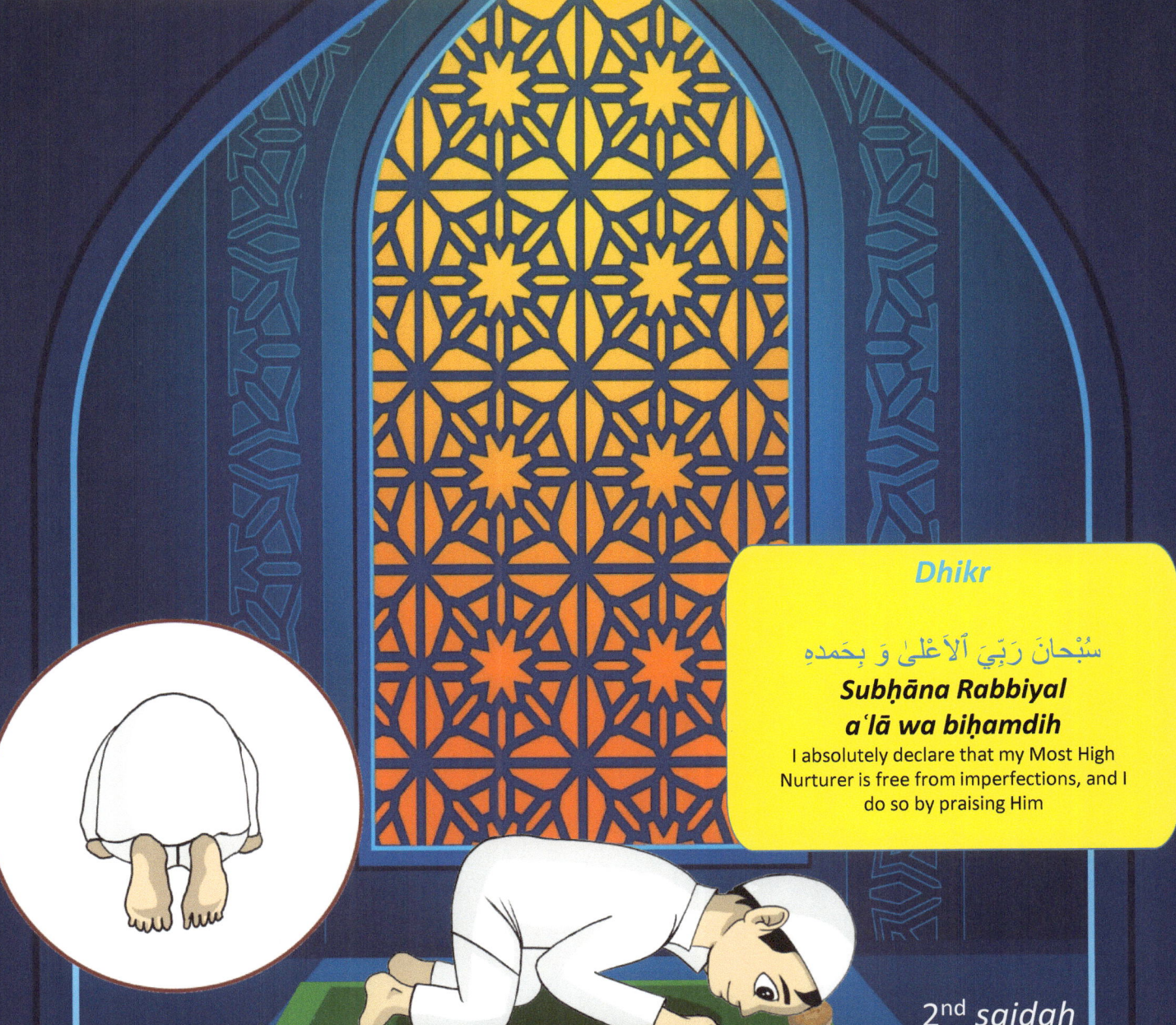

2nd *sajdah*

- After the 2nd *sajdah*, sit in the recommended position
- Keep body still
- Recommended to say *Allahu Akbar*
- Now recite *tashahhud* (testifying)
- After *tashahhud* recite the *taslīm* (salutation)

Tashahhud

اشْهَدُ اَنْ لاَاِلٰهَ اِلاَّ اللهُ وَحْدَهُ لاَشَرِيكَ لَهُ

Ashhadu a(n)l lā ilāha illa lāhu waḥdahu lā sharīka lah
All praise is for Allah, I testify that there is no god but Allah, He is alone, for whom there is no partner

وَ أَشْهَدُ أَنَّ مُحَمَّداً عَبْدُهُ وَ رَسُولُه

Wa ashhadu anna Muḥammadan 'abduhu wa rasūluh
And I testify that Muḥammad is His servant and His messenger

أَلَّلٰهُمَّ صَلِّ عَلىٰ مُحَمَّدٍ وَ آلِ مُحَمَّد

Allahumma Ṣalli 'alā Muḥammadi(n)w wa āli Muḥammad
O Allah! Bless Muḥammad and the progeny of Muḥammad

Taslīm

اَلسَّلَامُ عَلَيْكَ اَيُّها اَلنَّبِيُّ وَ رَحْمَةُ اللهِ وَ بَرَكَاتُه

Assalāmu 'alayka ayyuhan nabiyyu wa raḥmatullāhi wa barakātuh
Peace be upon you O Prophet, and Allah's mercy and His blessings (be upon you too)

اَلسَّلَامُ عَلَيْنا وَ عَلىٰ عِبَادِ اللهِ الصَّالِحِينَ

Assalāmu 'alaynā wa 'alā 'ibādillāhiṣ ṣaliḥīn
Peace be upon us and upon the righteous servants of Allah

السَّلَامُ عَلَيْكُمْ وَ رَحْمَةُ اللهِ وَ بَرَكَاتُه

Assalāmu 'alaykum wa raḥmatul lāhi wa barakātuh
Peace be upon you all, and Allah's mercy and His blessings (be upon you too)

DONE

Now you have completed *Ṣalāt al-Fajr*.
Well done!

After prayers it is recommended to say *dhikr* and *duas*.
Highly recommended to say the *dhikr* of Sayyida Fāṭimah (as).

Dhikr of Sayyida Fāṭimah (as)

اللهُ أكبَر

***Allahu Akbar* x 34**
Allah is greater (than what He is described as)

الْحَمْدُ لِلّهِ

***Alḥamdu lillāh* x 33**
All praise is for Allah

سُبْحانَ اللهِ

***Subḥānal lāh* x 33**
I declare that Allah is free from imperfections

HOW TO PRAY ṢALĀT AL – ẒUHR

4 x *rakʿahs*

- Focus on what you are doing
- Focus on who you are standing in front of
- Block out distractions
- Put your heart and mind into prayer
- Face the Kaʿbah
- Stand up straight

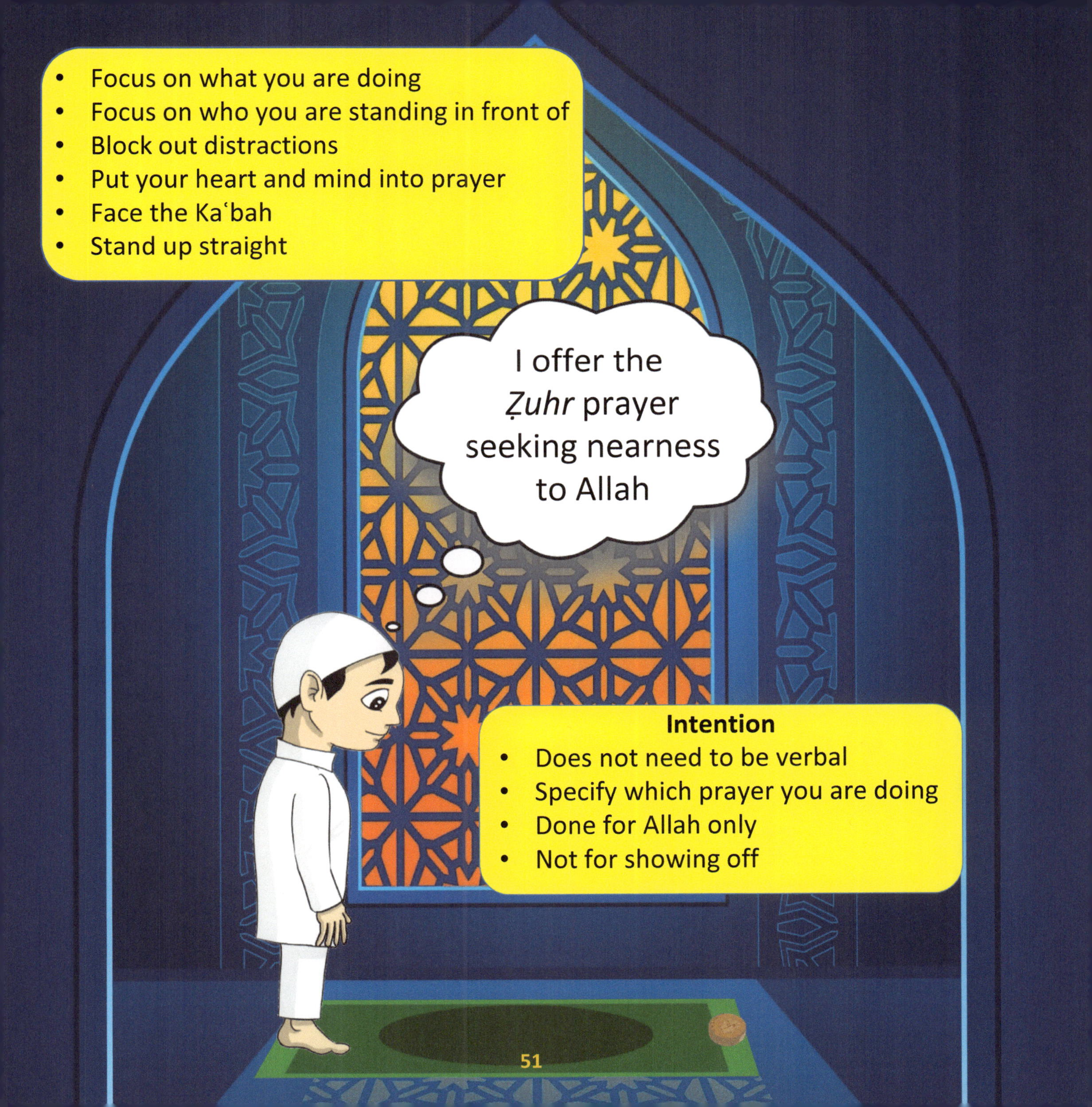

I offer the *Ẓuhr* prayer seeking nearness to Allah

Intention

- Does not need to be verbal
- Specify which prayer you are doing
- Done for Allah only
- Not for showing off

Lift both hands up to your ears and say *Allahu Akbar*

(Allah is greater than what He is described as)

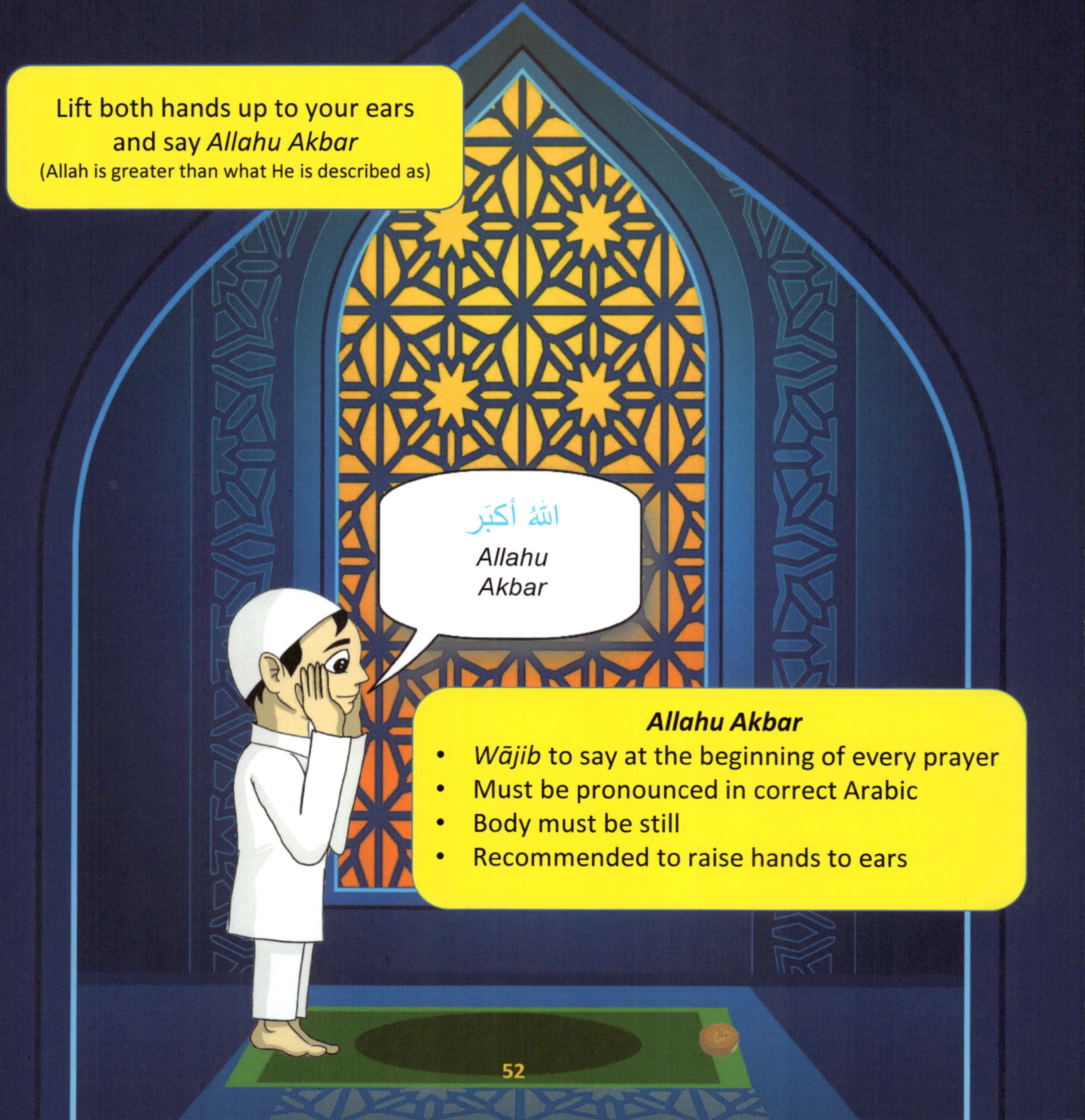

Allahu Akbar

- *Wājib* to say at the beginning of every prayer
- Must be pronounced in correct Arabic
- Body must be still
- Recommended to raise hands to ears

- Remain standing
- Recite Sūrah al-Fātiḥah
- Recite in clear Arabic
- **Males and Females recite soft (whisper)**
- Recommended to recite the '*Bismillāh*' aloud

بِسْمِ اللَّـهِ الرَّحْمَـٰنِ الرَّحِيمِ

Bismil lāhir Raḥmānir Raḥīm

I start in the name of Allah, the All Merciful towards all existents, The Kindest towards believers

الْحَمْدُ لِلَّـهِ رَبِّ الْعَالَمِينَ

Alḥamdu lillāhi Rabbil ʿālamīn

All praise and thanks are (just) for Allah, The Nurturer of all worlds

الرَّحْمَـٰنِ الرَّحِيمِ

Arraḥmānir Raḥīm

The All Merciful towards all existents, The Kindest towards believers

مَالِكِ يَوْمِ الدِّينِ

Māliki yawmid dīn

The (only real) Owner of everything (and the only authority) on Judgement day

إِيَّاكَ نَعْبُدُ وَإِيَّاكَ نَسْتَعِينُ

Iyyāka naʿbudu wa iyyāka nastaʿīn

((O Allah!)) You (and only You) we worship and You (and only You) we seek help from (as the independent deity)

اهْدِنَا الصِّرَاطَ الْمُسْتَقِيمَ

Ihdinaṣ ṣirāṭal mustaqīm

Guide (and take) us to the right Path

صِرَاطَ الَّذِينَ أَنْعَمْتَ عَلَيْهِمْ
غَيْرِ الْمَغْضُوبِ عَلَيْهِمْ وَلَا الضَّالِّينَ

Ṣirāṭal ladhīna anʿamta ʿalayhim ghayril maghḍūbi ʿalayhim wa laḍ ḍāllīn

The path of those whom You have bestowed your Blessings upon. Not of those who have earned Your wrath and not (of) those who have gone astray

- Remain standing
- Recite in clear Arabic
- Recite another *Sūrah*
- **Males and Females recite soft (whisper)**
- Recommended to recite the '*Bismillāh*' aloud

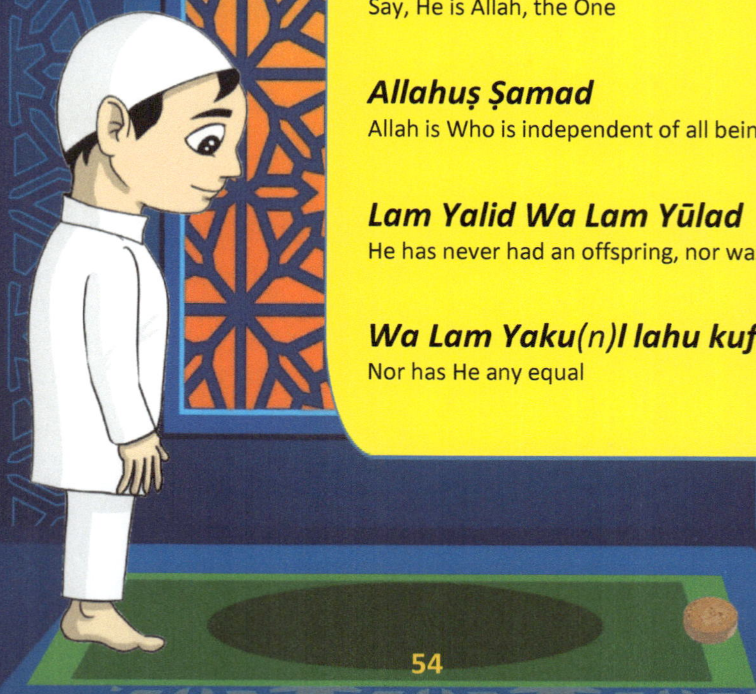

بِسْمِ اللَّـهِ الرَّحْمَـٰنِ الرَّحِيمِ

Bismil lāhir Raḥmānir Raḥīm

I start in the name of Allah, the All Merciful towards all existents, The Kindest towards believers

قُلْ هُوَ اللَّـهُ أَحَدٌ

Qul Huwal lāhu aḥad

Say, He is Allah, the One

اللَّـهُ الصَّمَدُ

Allahuṣ Ṣamad

Allah is Who is independent of all beings

لَمْ يَلِدْ وَلَمْ يُولَدْ

Lam Yalid Wa Lam Yūlad

He has never had an offspring, nor was He born

وَلَمْ يَكُن لَّهُ كُفُوًا أَحَدٌ

Wa Lam Yaku(n)l lahu kufuwan aḥad

Nor has He any equal

Lift both hands up to your ears and say *Allahu Akbar*
(Allah is greater than what He is described as)

Rukūʿ

Bowing

- Bend forward and place hands on your knees
- Recite in correct Arabic
- Remain steady
- While in this position recite a *dhikr* (glorification)
- Also recommended to say:

اللّهُمّ صَلّ عَلَى مُحَمّدٍ وَآلِ مُحَمّدٍ

Allahumma Ṣalli ʿalā Muḥammadi(n)w wa āli Muḥammad

(O Allah, Bless Muḥammad and the progeny of Muḥammad)

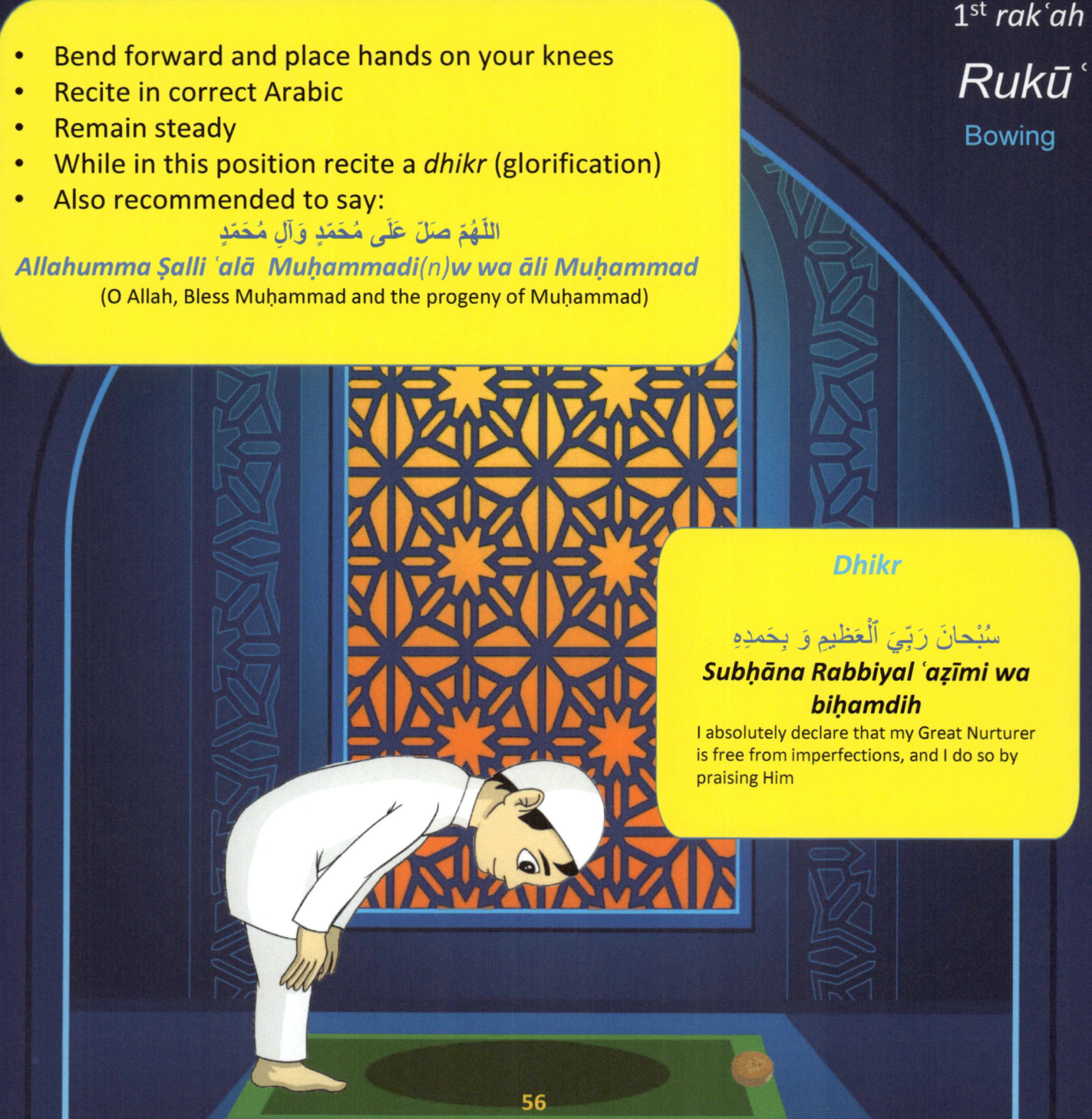

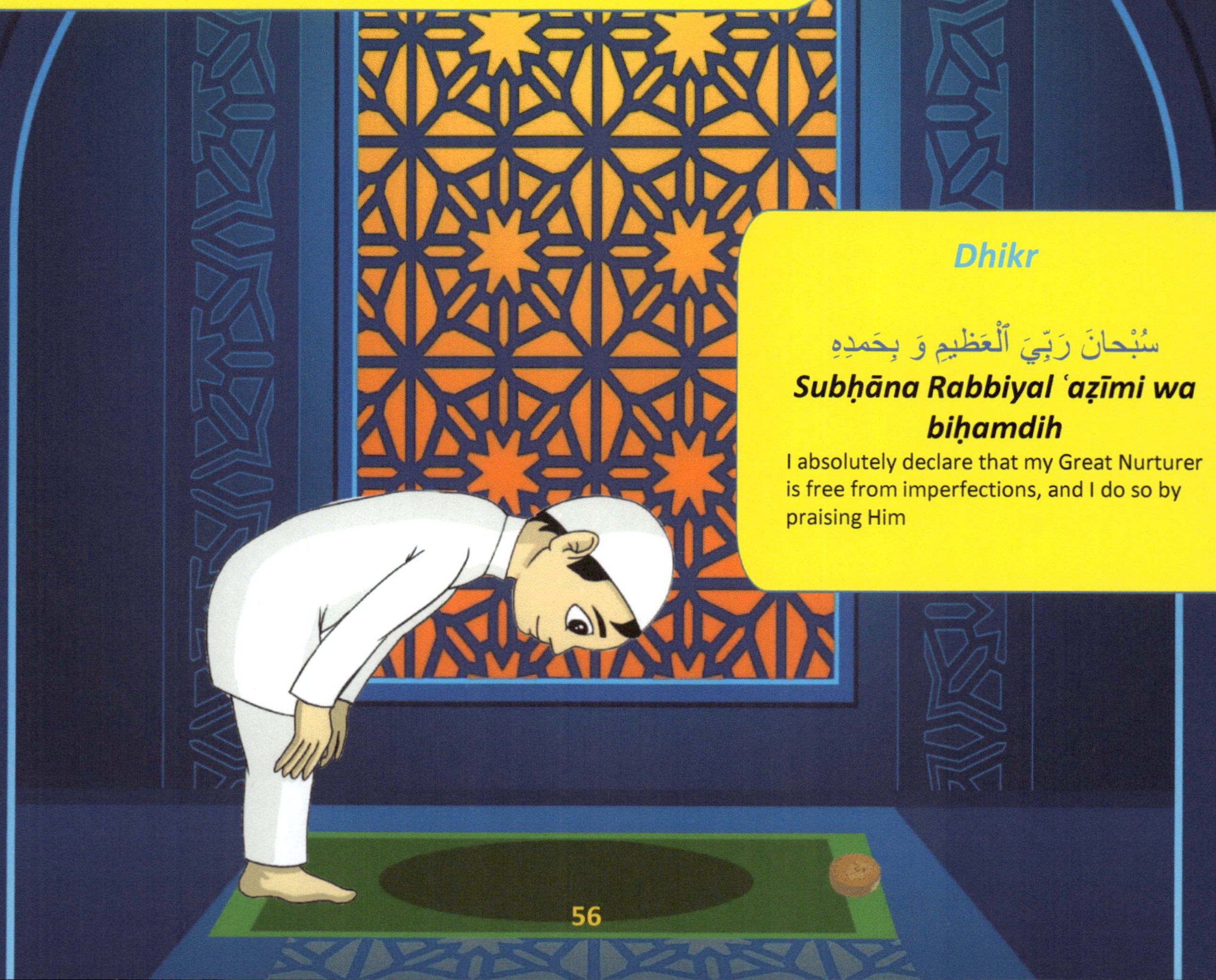

Dhikr

سُبْحانَ رَبِّيَ ٱلْعَظِيمِ وَ بِحَمدِهِ

Subḥāna Rabbiyal ʿaẓīmi wa biḥamdih

I absolutely declare that my Great Nurturer is free from imperfections, and I do so by praising Him

- Stand up straight and still
- Recommended to say ***Samiʿal lāhu liman ḥamidah***
  (Allah hears the one who praises Him)
- Then say *Allahu Akbar*
  (Allah is greater than what He is described as)

سَمِعَ اللهُ لِمَن حَمدَه
Samiʿal lāhu liman ḥamidah
الله أكبر
Allahu Akbar

- Place your forehead on the ground in humility
- Place both palms of your hands, both knees and both big toes on the ground
- Remain still
- Recommended for women to place their elbows on the ground
- Recite in correct Arabic
- While in this position recite a *dhikr* (glorification)
- Also recommended to say:

اللّٰهُمَّ صَلِّ عَلَىٰ مُحَمَّدٍ وَآلِ مُحَمَّدٍ

Allahumma Ṣalli ʿalā Muḥammadi(n)w wa āli Muḥammad
(O Allah, Bless Muḥammad and the progeny of Muḥammad)

You must perform *sajdah* on earth and of those things that grow from the earth but neither edible nor worn, such as wood or leaves.
The best thing to perform *sajdah* on is the soil of Imam Hussein (as).

Dhikr

سُبْحَانَ رَبِّيَ ٱلْأَعْلَىٰ وَ بِحَمْدِهِ

Subḥāna Rabbiyal aʿlā wa biḥamdih
I absolutely declare that my Most High Nurturer is free from imperfections, and I do so by praising Him

1st *sajdah*

- After the 1st *sajdah*, it is recommended to sit with the top part of the right foot on the sole of the left foot
- Recommended to place hands on thighs
- Recommended to say *Allahu Akbar*
- Recommended to also say :

اَستَغفِرُ اللهَ رَبِّي وَاتُوبُ اِلَيه

Astaghfirul lāha rabbī wa atūbu ilayh

(I seek forgiveness from Allah, My Nurturer, and I turn to Him in repentance)

1st *rakʿah*

- Place your forehead on the ground in humility
- Perform the 2nd *sajdah* in the same manner as the first

Dhikr

سُبْحانَ رَبِّيَ ٱلاَعْلىٰ وَ بِحَمدهِ

Subḥāna Rabbiyal aʿlā wa biḥamdih

I absolutely declare that my Most High Nurturer is free from imperfections, and I do so by praising Him

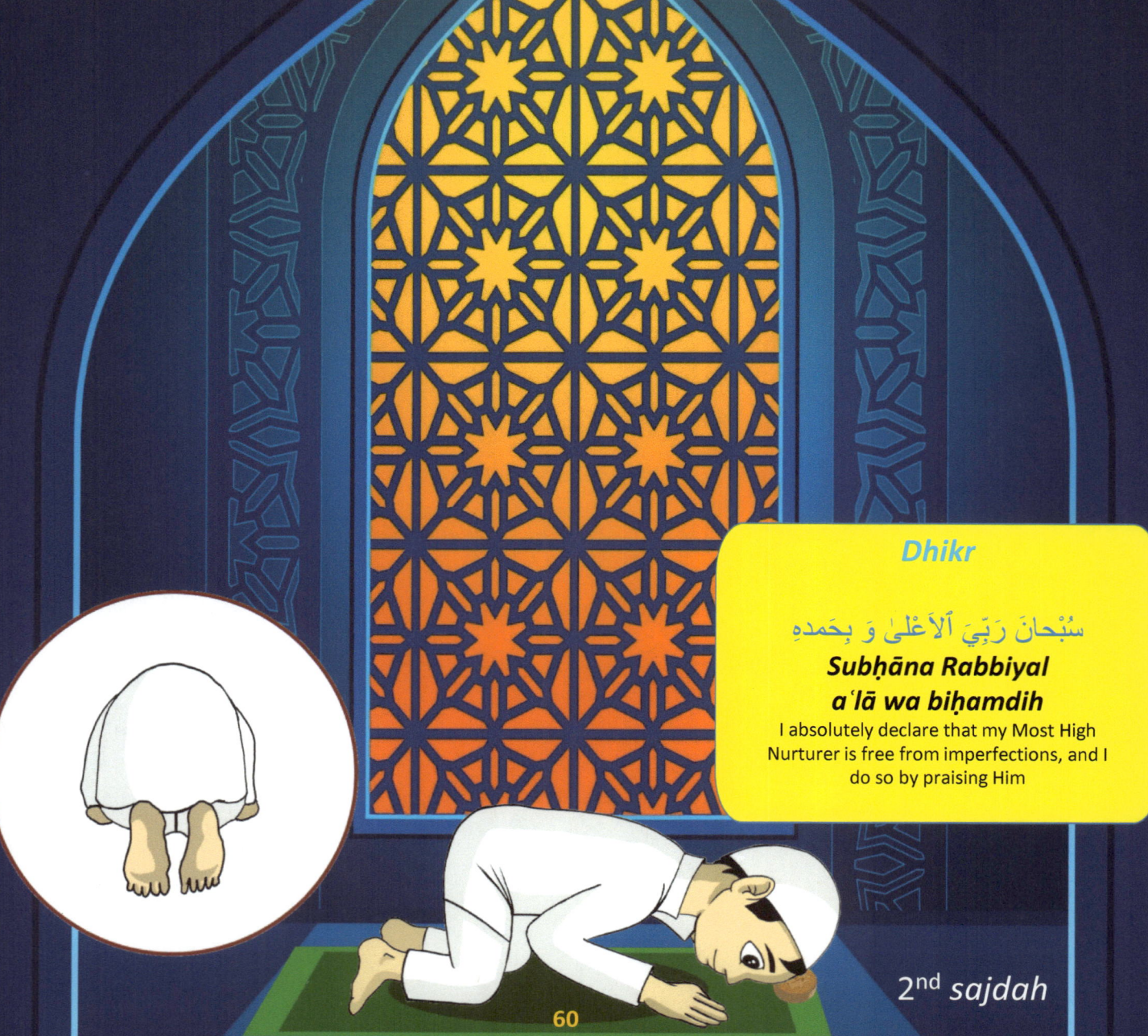

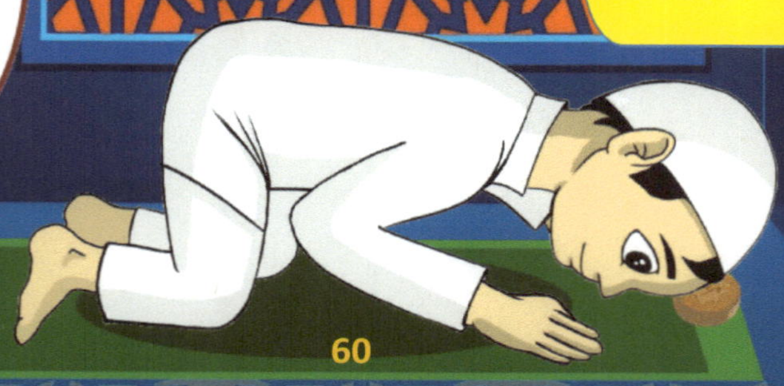

2nd *sajdah*

- After the 2nd *sajdah*, sit in the recommended position
- Keep body still
- Recommended to say *Allahu Akbar*

1ˢᵗ *rak'ah*

الله أكبَر

Allahu Akbar

- Stand back up
- While getting up it is recommended to say:

Biḥawlil lāhi wa quwwatihi aqūmu wa aqʻud
(I stand and sit by the strength of Allah and by His power)

بِحَولِ اللهِ وَ قُوَّتِهِ أَقُومُ وَ أَقْعُدُ
Biḥawlil lāhi wa quwwatihi aqūmu wa aqʿud

- Remain standing
- Recite Sūrah al-Fātiḥah
- Recite in clear Arabic
- **Males and Females recite soft (whisper)**
- Recommended to recite the '*Bismillāh*' aloud

بِسْمِ اللَّـهِ الرَّحْمَـٰنِ الرَّحِيمِ

Bismil lāhir Raḥmānir Raḥīm

I start in the name of Allah, the All Merciful towards all existents, The Kindest towards believers

الْحَمْدُ لِلَّـهِ رَبِّ الْعَالَمِينَ

Alḥamdu lillāhi Rabbil ʿālamīn

All praise and thanks are (just) for Allah, The Nurturer of all worlds

الرَّحْمَـٰنِ الرَّحِيمِ

Arraḥmānir Raḥīm

The All Merciful towards all existents, The Kindest towards believers

مَالِكِ يَوْمِ الدِّينِ

Māliki yawmid dīn

The (only real) Owner of everything (and the only authority) on Judgement day

إِيَّاكَ نَعْبُدُ وَإِيَّاكَ نَسْتَعِينُ

Iyyāka naʿbudu wa iyyāka nastaʿīn

((O Allah!)) You (and only You) we worship and You (and only You) we seek help from (as the independent deity)

اهْدِنَا الصِّرَاطَ الْمُسْتَقِيمَ

Ihdinaṣ ṣirāṭal mustaqīm

Guide (and take) us to the right Path

صِرَاطَ الَّذِينَ أَنْعَمْتَ عَلَيْهِمْ
غَيْرِ الْمَغْضُوبِ عَلَيْهِمْ وَلَا الضَّالِّينَ

Ṣirāṭal ladhīna anʿamta ʿalayhim ghayril maghḍūbi ʿalayhim wa laḍ ḍāllīn

The path of those whom You have bestowed your Blessings upon. Not of those who have earned Your wrath and not (of) those who have gone astray

- Remain standing
- Recite in clear Arabic
- Recite another Sūrah
- **Males and Females recite soft (whisper)**
- Recommended to recite the '*Bismillāh*' aloud

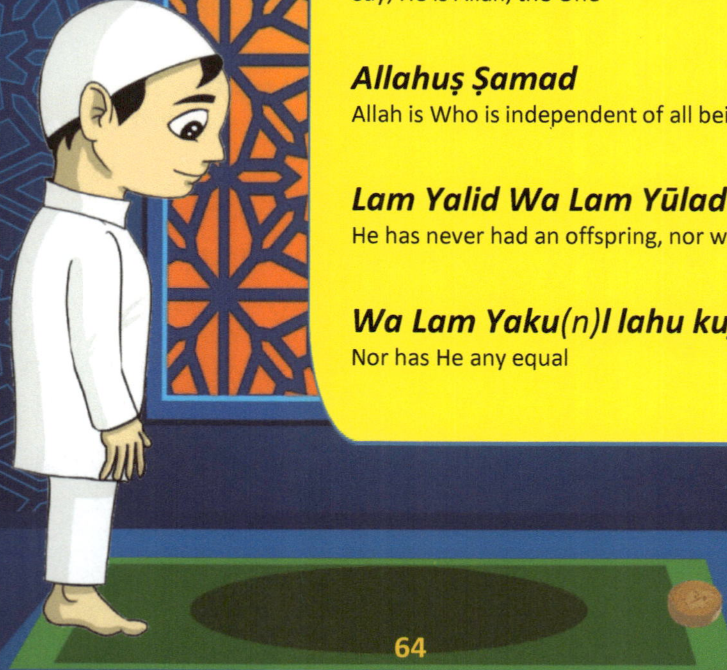

بِسْمِ اللَّـهِ الرَّحْمَـٰنِ الرَّحِيمِ

Bismil lāhir Raḥmānir Raḥīm

I start in the name of Allah, the All Merciful towards all existents, The Kindest towards believers

قُلْ هُوَ اللَّـهُ أَحَدٌ

Qul Huwal lāhu aḥad

Say, He is Allah, the One

اللَّـهُ الصَّمَدُ

Allahuṣ Ṣamad

Allah is Who is independent of all beings

لَمْ يَلِدْ وَلَمْ يُولَدْ

Lam Yalid Wa Lam Yūlad

He has never had an offspring, nor was He born

وَلَمْ يَكُن لَّهُ كُفُوًا أَحَدٌ

Wa Lam Yaku(n)l lahu kufuwan aḥad

Nor has He any equal

- It is recommended to perform *qunūt* before *Rukūʿ* in 2nd *rakʿah*
- Place hands in front of your face with palms facing the sky and both hands and fingers next to each other
- You can say any *dhikr*
- After *dhikr* say *Allahu Akbar*

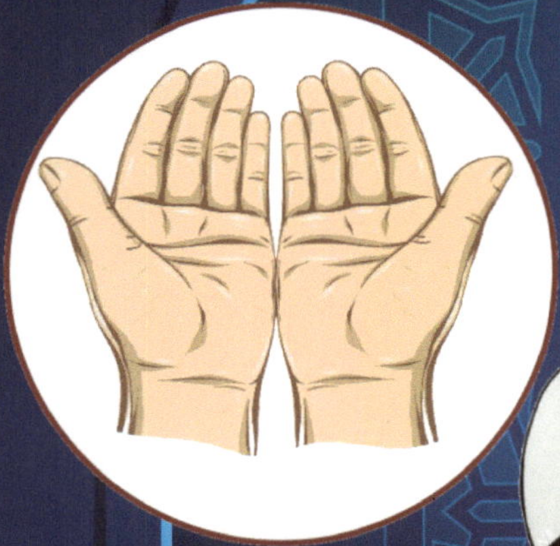

Dhikr

رَبَّنَا أَفْرِغْ عَلَيْنَا صَبْرًا

Rabbanā afrigh ʿalaynā ṣabrā,
Our Nurturer! Shower us with patience,

وَثَبِّتْ أَقْدَامَنَا

wa thabbit aqdāmanā,
And make us stand firm,

وَانصُرْنَا عَلَى الْقَوْمِ الْكَافِرِينَ

wan ṣurnā ʿalal qawmil kāfirīn
And help us against the coverers of the truth

Perform the *rukūʿ* and the two *sajdahs*
2nd *rakʿah*
1
2
3
4
5
6

- After the 2nd *sajdah* remain seated
- Keep body still
- Recommended to say *Allahu Akbar*
- Now recite *tashahhud*

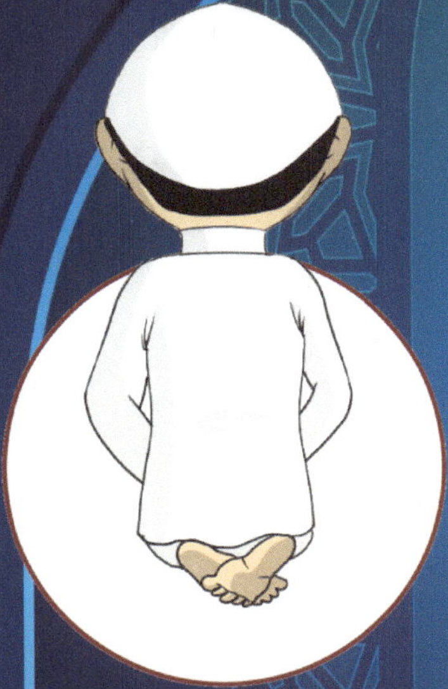

Tashahhud

اشْهَدُ اَنْ لااِلٰهَ اِلاَّ اللّٰهُ وَحْدَهُ لاشَرِيكَ لَهُ

Ashhadu a(n)l lā ilāha illa lāhu waḥdahu lā sharīka lah

All praise is for Allah, I testify that there is no god but Allah, He is alone, for whom there is no partner

وَ أَشْهَدُ أَنَّ مُحَمَّداً عَبْدُهُ وَ رَسُولُه

Wa ashhadu anna Muḥammadan ʿabduhu wa rasūluh

And I testify that Muḥammad is His servant and His messenger

أَللّٰهُمَّ صَلِّ عَلىٰ مُحَمَّدٍ وَ آلِ مُحَمَّد

Allahumma Ṣalli ʿalā Muḥammadi(n)w wa āli Muḥammad

O Allah! Bless Muḥammad and the progeny of Muḥammad

Tasbīḥāt al-arbaʿah

- Stand back up for the 3rd *rakʿah*
- Recite the 4 *tasbiḥs* x 1, but better to say it 3 times
- **Males and Females recite soft (whisper)**

After the 4 *tasbiḥs* it is recommended to also say :

اَستَغفِرُ اللهَ رَبِّي وَاتُوبُ اِلَيه

Astaghfirul lāha rabbī wa atūbu ilayh

(I seek forgiveness from Allah, My Nurturer, and I turn to Him in repentance)

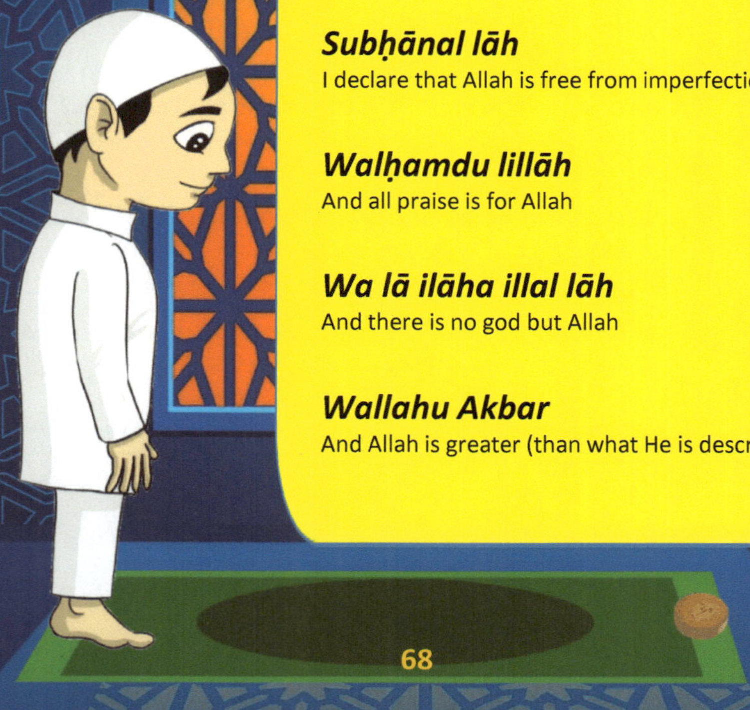

Tasbiḥāt al-arbaʿah

سُبْحَانَ اللهِ

Subḥānal lāh

I declare that Allah is free from imperfections

وَ الْحَمْدُ لِلهِ

Walḥamdu lillāh

And all praise is for Allah

وَ لاَ إِلهَ إلاَّ اللهُ

Wa lā ilāha illal lāh

And there is no god but Allah

وَ اللهُ أكْبَرُ

Wallahu Akbar

And Allah is greater (than what He is described as)

Perform the *rukūʿ* and the two *sajdahs*
3rd *rakʿah*
1
2
3
4
5
6

Tasbīḥāt al-arbaʿah

- Stand back up for the 4th *rakʿah*
- Recite the 4 *tasbiḥs* x 1, but better to say it 3 times
- **Males and Females recite soft (whisper)**

After the 4 *tasbiḥs* it is recommended to also say :

اَستَغفِرُ اللهَ رَبِّي وَاتُوبُ اِلَيه

Astaghfirul lāha rabbī wa atūbu ilayh

(I seek forgiveness from Allah, My Nurturer, and I turn to Him in repentance)

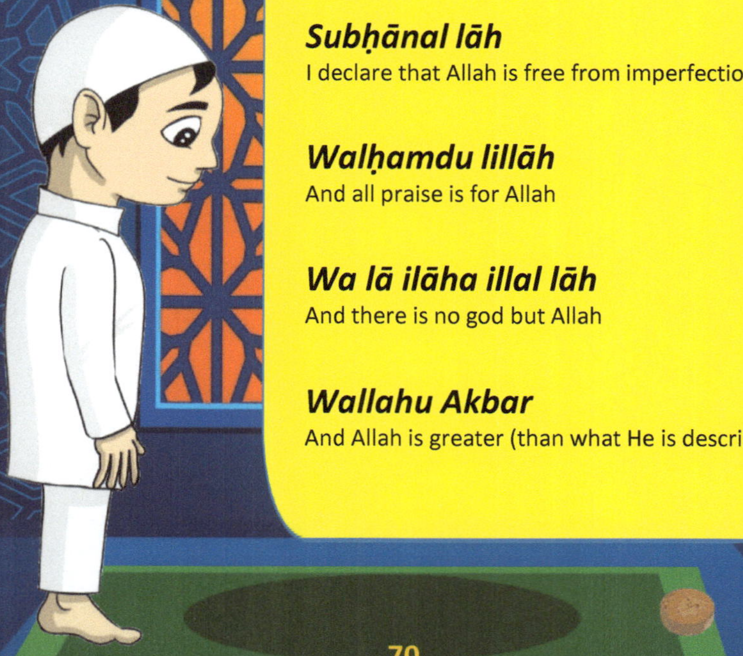

Tasbiḥāt al-arbaʿah

سُبْحَانَ اللهِ

Subḥānal lāh

I declare that Allah is free from imperfections

وَ الْحَمْدُ لِلهِ

Walḥamdu lillāh

And all praise is for Allah

وَ لاَ إِلهَ إلاَّ اللهُ

Wa lā ilāha illal lāh

And there is no god but Allah

وَ اللهُ أكْبَرُ

Wallahu Akbar

And Allah is greater (than what He is described as)

Perform the rukūʿ and the two sajdahs
4th rakʿah
1
2
3
4
5
6

4th *rakʿah*

- After the 2nd *sajdah* remain seated
- Now recite *tashahhud*
- After *tashahhud* recite the *taslīm*

Tashahhud

اشْهَدُ اَنْ لااِلٰهَ اِلاَّ اللهُ وَحْدَهُ لاشَرِيكَ لَهُ

Ashhadu a(n)l lā ilāha illa lāhu waḥdahu lā sharīka lah

All praise is for Allah, I testify that there is no god but Allah, He is alone, for whom there is no partner

وَ أَشْهَدُ أَنَّ مُحَمَّداً عَبْدُهُ وَ رَسُولُه

Wa ashhadu anna Muḥammadan ʿabduhu wa rasūluh

And I testify that Muḥammad is His servant and His messenger

اَللّٰهُمَّ صَلِّ عَلٰى مُحَمَّدٍ وَ آلِ مُحَمَّد

Allahumma Ṣalli ʿalā Muḥammadi(n)w wa āli Muḥammad

O Allah! Bless Muḥammad and the progeny of Muḥammad

Taslīm

اَلسَّلامُ عَلَيْكَ اَيُّها اَلنَّبِيُّ وَ رَحْمَةُ اللهِ وَ بَرَكاتُه

Assalāmu ʿalayka ayyuhan nabiyyu wa raḥmatullāhi wa barakātuh

Peace be upon you O Prophet, and Allah's mercy and His blessings (be upon you too)

اَلسَّلامُ عَلَينا وَ عَلىٰ عِبادِ اللهِ الصّالِحِينَ

Assalāmu ʿalaynā wa ʿalā ʿibādillāhiṣ ṣaliḥīn

Peace be upon us and upon the righteous servants of Allah

السَّلامُ عَلَيْكُمْ وَ رَحْمَةُ اللهِ وَ بَرَكاتُه

Assalāmu ʿalaykum wa raḥmatul lāhi wa barakātuh

Peace be upon you all, and Allah's mercy and His blessings (be upon you too)

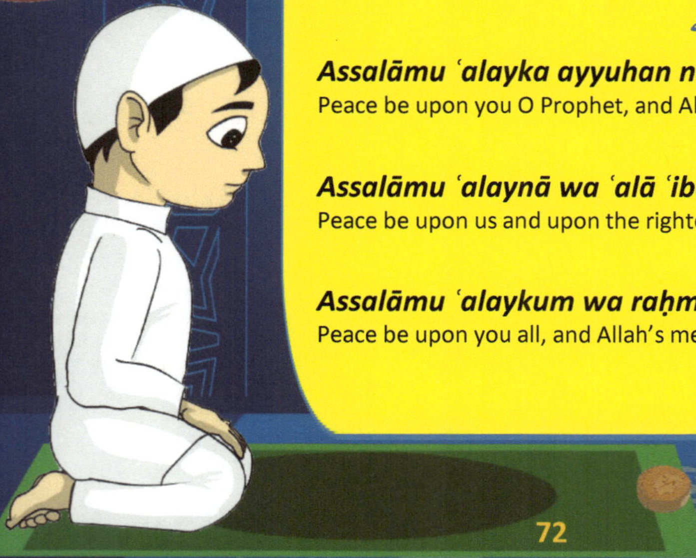

DONE

Now you have completed *Ṣalāt al-Ẓuhr*. Well done!

After prayers it is recommended to say *dhikr* and *duas*.
Highly recommended to say the *dhikr* of Sayyida Fāṭimah (as).

Dhikr of Sayyida Fāṭimah (as)

اللهُ أكبَر

***Allahu Akbar* x 34**
Allah is greater (than what He is described as)

الْحَمْدُ لِلّهِ

***Alḥamdu lillāh* x 33**
All praise is for Allah

سُبْحانَ اللهِ

***Subḥānal lāh* x 33**
I declare that Allah is free from imperfections

HOW TO PRAY ṢALĀT AL – ʿAṢR

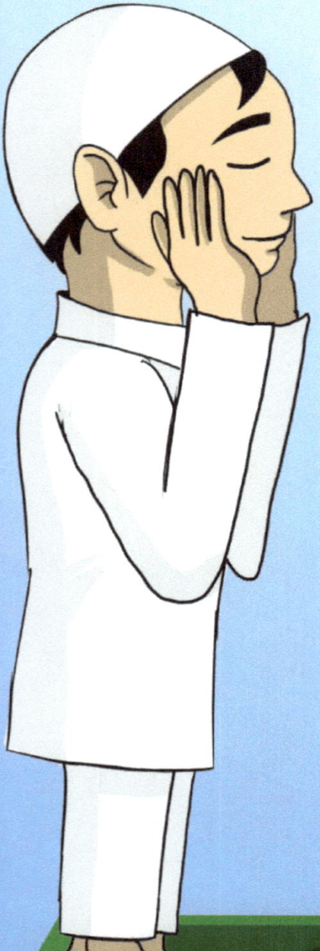

4 x rakʿahs

Perform *Ṣalāt al-ʿAṣr* exactly like *Ṣalāt al-Ẓuhr* except **with the intention of *ʿAṣr* prayers** at its prescribed time.

I offer the *ʿAṣr* prayer seeking nearness to Allah

DONE

Now you have completed *Ṣalāt al-ʿAṣr*. Well done!

After prayers it is recommended to say *dhikr* and *duas*.
Highly recommended to say the *dhikr* of Sayyida Fāṭimah (as).

Dhikr of Sayyida Fāṭimah (as)

اللهُ أكبَر

***Allahu Akbar* x 34**
Allah is greater (than what He is described as)

الْحَمْدُ لِلّهِ

***Alḥamdu lillāh* x 33**
All praise is for Allah

سُبْحانَ اللّهِ

***Subḥānal lāh* x 33**
I declare that Allah is free from imperfections

HOW TO PRAY ṢALĀT AL - MAGHRIB

3 x *rakʿahs*

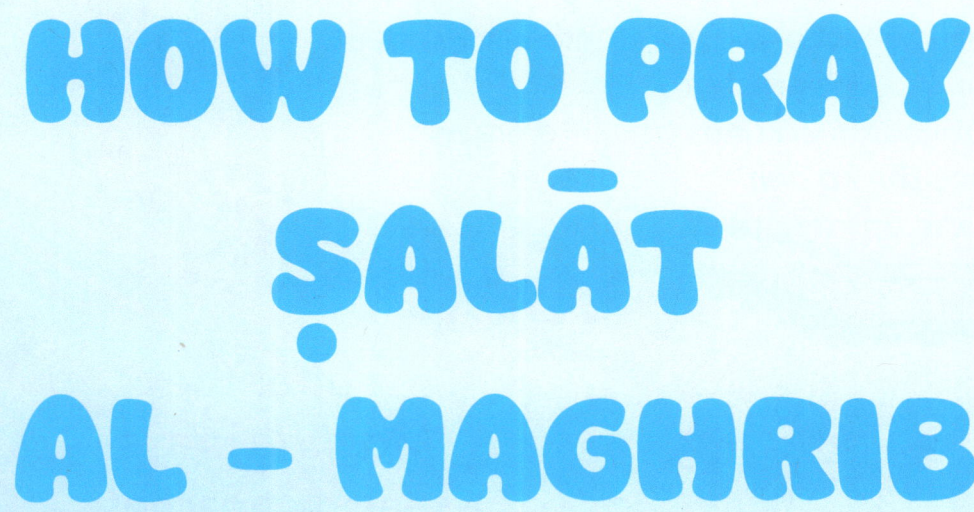

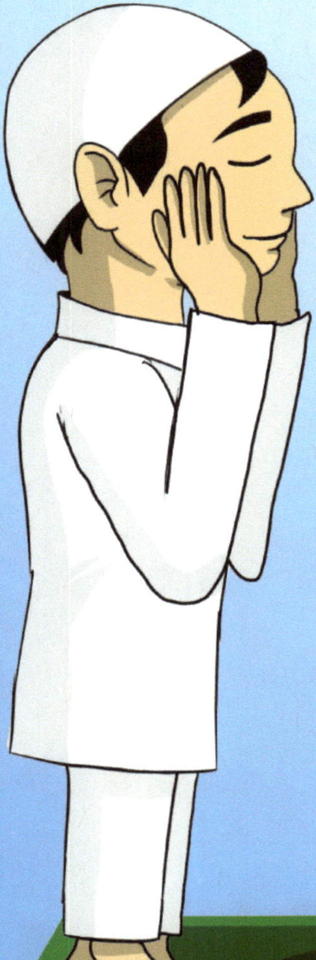

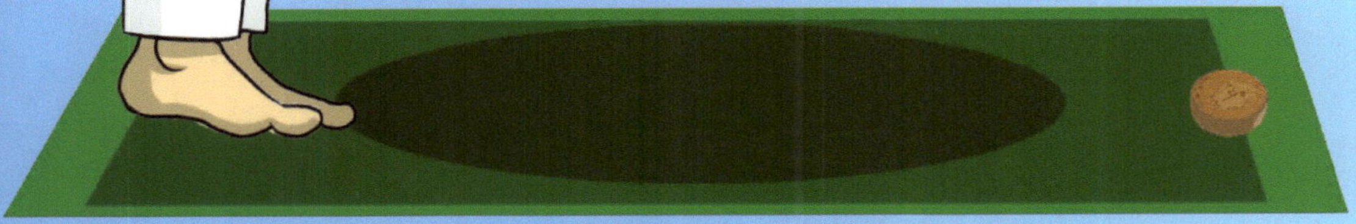

- Focus on what you are doing
- Focus on who you are standing in front of
- Block out distractions
- Put your heart and mind into prayer
- Face the *Kaʿbah*
- Stand up straight

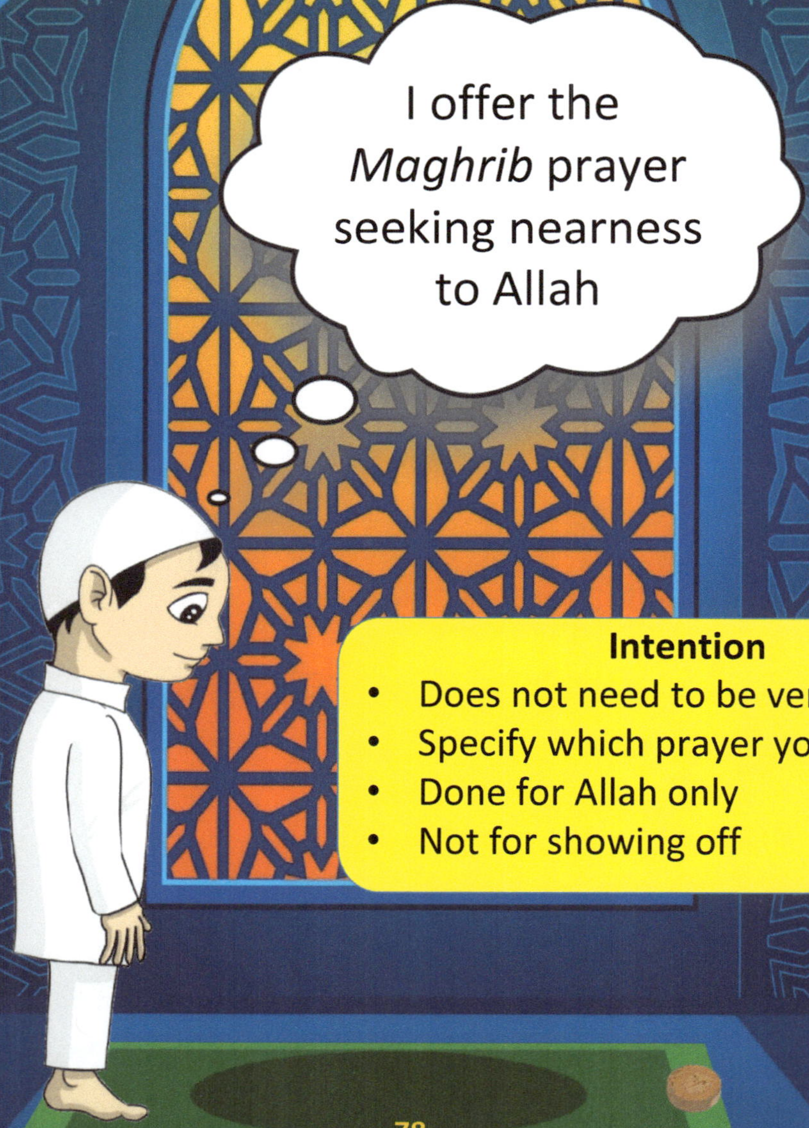

I offer the *Maghrib* prayer seeking nearness to Allah

Intention

- Does not need to be verbal
- Specify which prayer you are doing
- Done for Allah only
- Not for showing off

Lift both hands up to your ears and say *Allahu Akbar*
(Allah is greater than what He is described as)

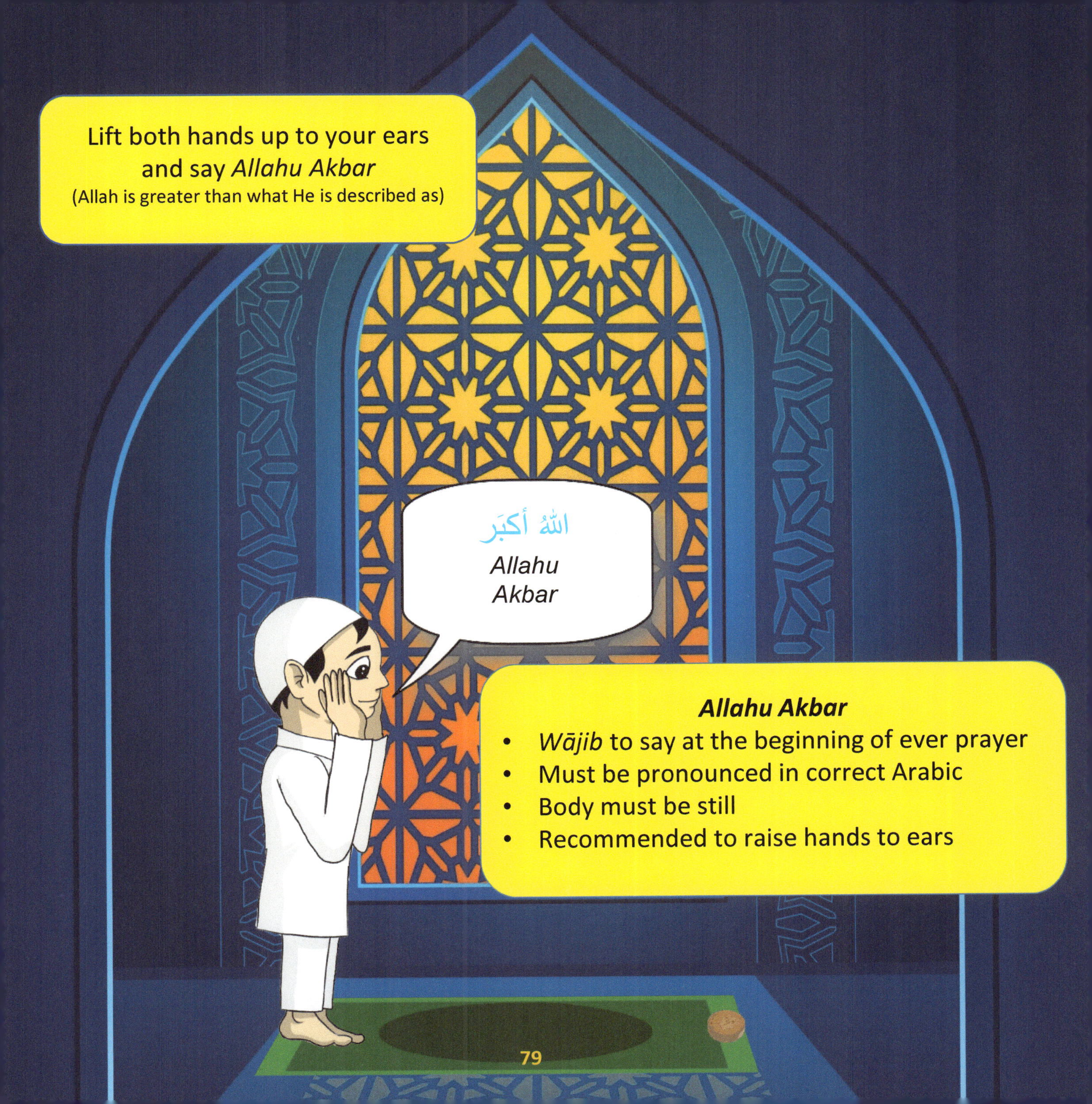

Allahu Akbar

- *Wājib* to say at the beginning of ever prayer
- Must be pronounced in correct Arabic
- Body must be still
- Recommended to raise hands to ears

- Remain standing
- Recite Sūrah al-Fātiḥah
- Recite in clear Arabic
- Males recite aloud
- Females recite aloud or soft, but recite soft in front of a *non-maḥram*

بِسْمِ اللَّـهِ الرَّحْمَـٰنِ الرَّحِيمِ

Bismil lāhir Raḥmānir Raḥīm

I start in the name of Allah, the All Merciful towards all existents, The Kindest towards believers

الْحَمْدُ لِلَّـهِ رَبِّ الْعَالَمِينَ

Alḥamdu lillāhi Rabbil ʿālamīn

All praise and thanks are (just) for Allah, The Nurturer of all worlds

الرَّحْمَـٰنِ الرَّحِيمِ

Arraḥmānir Raḥīm

The All Merciful towards all existents, The Kindest towards believers

مَالِكِ يَوْمِ الدِّينِ

Māliki yawmid dīn

The (only real) Owner of everything (and the only authority) on Judgement day

إِيَّاكَ نَعْبُدُ وَإِيَّاكَ نَسْتَعِينُ

Iyyāka naʿbudu wa iyyāka nastaʿīn

((O Allah!)) You (and only You) we worship and You (and only You) we seek help from (as the independent deity)

اهْدِنَا الصِّرَاطَ الْمُسْتَقِيمَ

Ihdinaṣ ṣirāṭal mustaqīm

Guide (and take) us to the right Path

صِرَاطَ الَّذِينَ أَنْعَمْتَ عَلَيْهِمْ
غَيْرِ الْمَغْضُوبِ عَلَيْهِمْ وَلَا الضَّالِّينَ

Ṣirāṭal ladhīna anʿamta ʿalayhim ghayril maghḍūbi ʿalayhim wa laḍ ḍāllīn

The path of those whom You have bestowed your Blessings upon. Not of those who have earned Your wrath and not (of) those who have gone astray

- Remain standing
- Recite in clear Arabic
- Recite another *Sūrah*
- Males recite aloud
- Females recite aloud or soft, but recite soft in front of a *non-maḥram*

بِسْمِ اللَّـهِ الرَّحْمَـٰنِ الرَّحِيمِ

Bismil lāhir Raḥmānir Raḥīm

I start in the name of Allah, the All Merciful towards all existents, The Kindest towards believers

قُلْ هُوَ اللَّـهُ أَحَدٌ

Qul Huwal lāhu aḥad

Say, He is Allah, the One

اللَّـهُ الصَّمَدُ

Allahuṣ Ṣamad

Allah is Who is independent of all beings

لَمْ يَلِدْ وَلَمْ يُولَدْ

Lam Yalid Wa Lam Yūlad

He has never had an offspring, nor was He born

وَلَمْ يَكُن لَّهُ كُفُوًا أَحَدٌ

Wa Lam Yaku*(n)*l lahu kufuwan aḥad

Nor has He any equal

1st *rakʿah*

Rukūʿ

Bowing

- Bend forward and place hands on your knees
- Recite in correct Arabic
- Remain steady
- While in this position recite a *dhikr* (glorification)
- Also recommended to say:

اللّهُمّ صَلّ عَلَى مُحَمّدٍ وَآلِ مُحَمّدٍ

Allahumma Ṣalli ʿalā Muḥammadi(n)w wa āli Muḥammad

(O Allah, Bless Muḥammad and the progeny of Muḥammad)

Dhikr

سُبْحانَ رَبِّيَ ٱلْعَظِيمِ وَ بِحَمدِهِ

Subḥāna Rabbiyal ʿaẓīmi wa biḥamdih

I absolutely declare that my Great Nurturer is free from imperfections, and I do so by praising Him

- Stand up straight and still
- Recommended to say ***Samiʿal lāhu liman ḥamidah***
  (Allah hears the one who praises Him)
- Then say *Allahu Akbar*
  (Allah is greater than what He is described as)

سَمِعَ اللهُ لِمَن حَمِدَه
Samiʿal lāhu liman ḥamidah
الله أكبر
Allahu Akbar

1st *rakʿah*

Sujūd

Prostrating

- Place your forehead on the ground in humility
- Place both palms of your hands, both knees and both big toes on the ground
- Remain still
- Recommended for women to place their elbows on the ground
- Recite in correct Arabic
- While in this position recite a *dhikr* (glorification)
- Also recommended to say:

اللّٰهُمَّ صَلِّ عَلَى مُحَمَّدٍ وَآلِ مُحَمَّدٍ

Allahumma Ṣalli ʿalā Muḥammadi(n)w wa āli Muḥammad

(O Allah, Bless Muḥammad and the progeny of Muḥammad)

You must perform *sajdah* on earth and of those things that grow from the earth but neither edible nor worn, such as wood or leaves.
The best thing to perform *sajdah* on is the soil of Imam Hussein (as).

Dhikr

سُبْحانَ رَبِّيَ ٱلأَعْلىٰ وَ بِحَمدِهِ

Subḥāna Rabbiyal aʿlā wa biḥamdih

I absolutely declare that my Most High Nurturer is free from imperfections, and I do so by praising Him

1st *sajdah*

- After the 1st *sajdah*, it is recommended to sit with the top part of the right foot on the sole of the left foot
- Recommended to place hands on thighs
- Recommended to say *Allahu Akbar*
- Recommended to also say :

اَستَغفِرُ اللهَ رَبِّي وَاتُوبُ اِلَيه

Astaghfirul lāha rabbī wa atūbu ilayh

(I seek forgiveness from Allah, My Nurturer, and I turn to Him in repentance)

- Place your forehead on the ground in humility
- Perform the 2nd *sajdah* in the same manner as the first

1st *rakʿah*

Sujūd

Prostrating

Dhikr

سُبْحانَ رَبِّيَ ٱلاَعْلىٰ وَ بِحَمدِهِ

Subḥāna Rabbiyal aʿlā wa biḥamdih

I absolutely declare that my Most High Nurturer is free from imperfections, and I do so by praising Him

2nd *sajdah*

- After the 2nd *sajdah*, sit in the recommended position
- Keep body still
- Recommended to say *Allahu Akbar*

- Stand back up
- While getting up it is recommended to say:
  Biḥawlil lāhi wa quwwatihi aqūmu wa aqʻud
  (I stand and sit by the strength of Allah and by His power)

بِحَوْلِ اللَّهِ وَ قُوَّتِهِ أَقُومُ وَ أَقْعُدُ

Biḥawlil lāhi wa quwwatihi aqūmu wa aqʻud

- Remain standing
- Recite Sūrah al-Fātiḥah
- Recite in clear Arabic
- Males recite aloud
- Females recite aloud or soft, but recite soft in front of a *non-maḥram*

بِسْمِ اللَّـهِ الرَّحْمَـٰنِ الرَّحِيمِ

Bismil lāhir Raḥmānir Raḥīm

I start in the name of Allah, the All Merciful towards all existents, The Kindest towards believers

الْحَمْدُ لِلَّـهِ رَبِّ الْعَالَمِينَ

Alḥamdu lillāhi Rabbil ʿālamīn

All praise and thanks are (just) for Allah, The Nurturer of all worlds

الرَّحْمَـٰنِ الرَّحِيمِ

Arraḥmānir Raḥīm

The All Merciful towards all existents, The Kindest towards believers

مَالِكِ يَوْمِ الدِّينِ

Māliki yawmid dīn

The (only real) Owner of everything (and the only authority) on Judgement day

إِيَّاكَ نَعْبُدُ وَإِيَّاكَ نَسْتَعِينُ

Iyyāka naʿbudu wa iyyāka nastaʿīn

((O Allah!)) You (and only You) we worship and You (and only You) we seek help from (as the independent deity)

اهْدِنَا الصِّرَاطَ الْمُسْتَقِيمَ

Ihdinaṣ ṣirāṭal mustaqīm

Guide (and take) us to the right Path

صِرَاطَ الَّذِينَ أَنْعَمْتَ عَلَيْهِمْ
غَيْرِ الْمَغْضُوبِ عَلَيْهِمْ وَلَا الضَّالِّينَ

Ṣirāṭal ladhīna anʿamta ʿalayhim ghayril maghḍūbi ʿalayhim wa laḍ ḍāllīn

The path of those whom You have bestowed your Blessings upon. Not of those who have earned Your wrath and not (of) those who have gone astray

- Remain standing
- Recite in clear Arabic
- Recite another *Sūrah*
- Males recite aloud
- Females recite aloud or soft, but recite soft in front of a *non-maḥram*

بِسْمِ اللَّـهِ الرَّحْمَـٰنِ الرَّحِيمِ

Bismil lāhir Raḥmānir Raḥīm

I start in the name of Allah, the All Merciful towards all existents, The Kindest towards believers

قُلْ هُوَ اللَّـهُ أَحَدٌ

Qul Huwal lāhu aḥad

Say, He is Allah, the One

اللَّـهُ الصَّمَدُ

Allahuṣ Ṣamad

Allah is Who is independent of all beings

لَمْ يَلِدْ وَلَمْ يُولَدْ

Lam Yalid Wa Lam Yūlad

He has never had an offspring, nor was He born

وَلَمْ يَكُن لَّهُ كُفُوًا أَحَدٌ

Wa Lam Yaku(n)l lahu kufuwan aḥad

Nor has He any equal

- It is recommended to perform *qunūt* before *rukūʿ* in 2nd *rakʿah*
- Place hands in front of your face with palms facing the sky and both hands and fingers next to each other
- You can say any *dhikr*
- After *dhikr* say *Allahu Akbar*

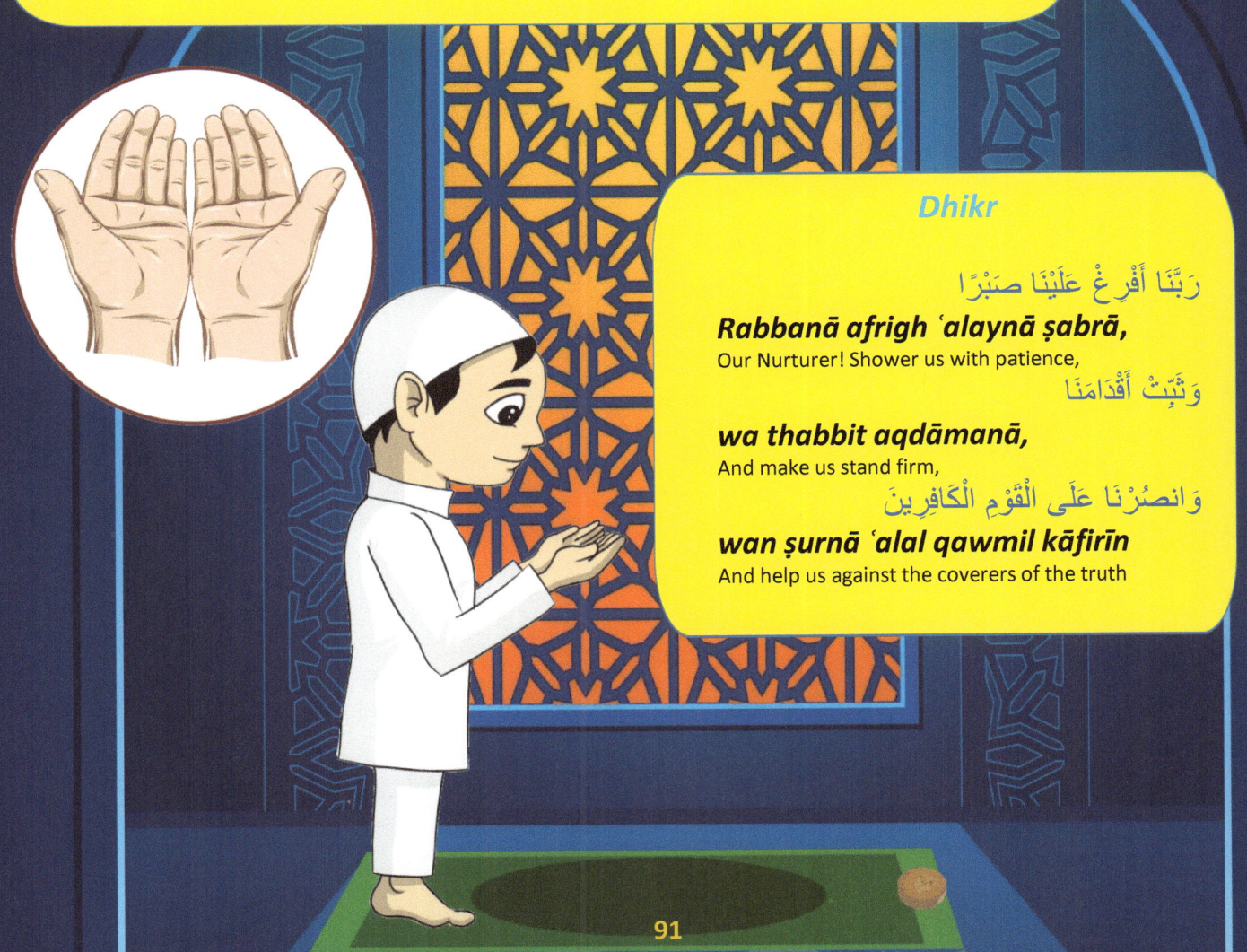

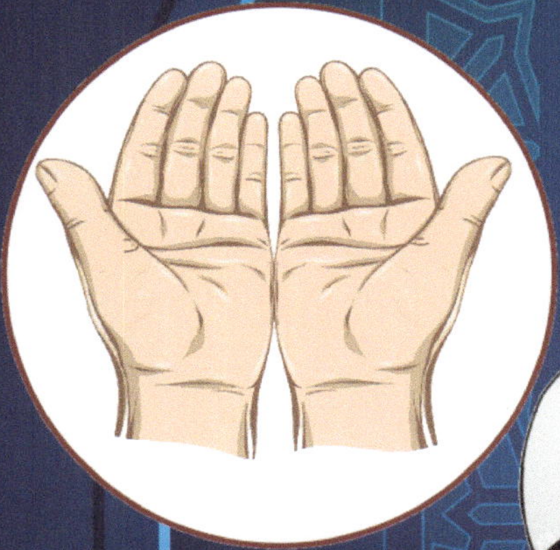

Dhikr

رَبَّنَا أَفْرِغْ عَلَيْنَا صَبْرًا

Rabbanā afrigh ʿalaynā ṣabrā,

Our Nurturer! Shower us with patience,

وَثَبِّتْ أَقْدَامَنَا

wa thabbit aqdāmanā,

And make us stand firm,

وَانصُرْنَا عَلَى الْقَوْمِ الْكَافِرِينَ

wan ṣurnā ʿalal qawmil kāfirīn

And help us against the coverers of the truth

Perform the *rukūʿ* and the two *sajdahs*
2nd *rakʿah*
1
2
3
4
5
6

- After the 2nd *sajdah* remain seated
- Keep body still
- Recommended to say *Allahu Akbar*
- Now recite *tashahhud* (testifying)

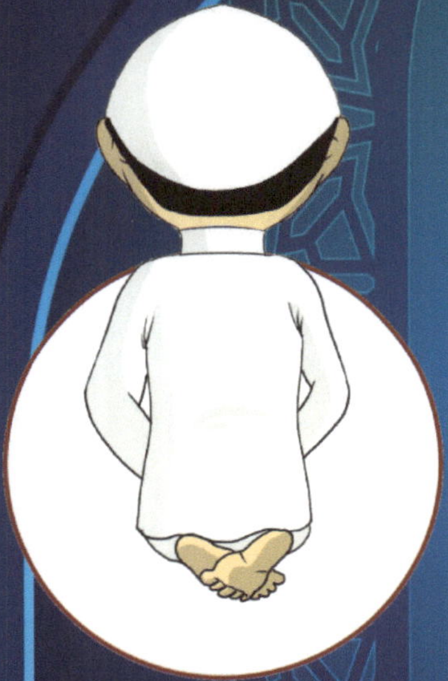

Tashahhud

اشْهَدُ اَنْ لاَاِلٰهَ اِلاَّ اللهُ وَحْدَهُ لاشَرِيكَ لَهُ

Ashhadu a(n)l lā ilāha illa lāhu waḥdahu lā sharīka lah

All praise is for Allah, I testify that there is no god but Allah, He is alone, for whom there is no partner

وَ أَشَهَدُ أَنَّ مُحَمَّداً عَبْدُهُ وَ رَسُولُه

Wa ashhadu anna Muḥammadan ʿabduhu wa rasūluh

And I testify that Muḥammad is His servant and His messenger

أَللّٰهُمَّ صَلِّ عَلىٰ مُحَمَّدٍ وَ آلِ مُحَمَّد

Allahumma Ṣalli ʿalā Muḥammadi(n)w wa āli Muḥammad

O Allah! Bless Muḥammad and the progeny of Muḥammad

3rd *rakʿah*

Tasbīḥāt al-arbaʿah

- Stand back up for the 3rd *rakʿah*
- Recite the 4 *tasbiḥs* x 1, but better to say it 3 times
- **Males and Females recite soft (whisper)**

After the 4 *tasbiḥs* it is recommended to also say :

اَستَغفِرُ اللهَ رَبِّي وَاَتُوبُ اِلَيه

Astaghfirul lāha rabbī wa atūbu ilayh

(I seek forgiveness from Allah, My Nurturer, and I turn to Him in repentance)

Tasbiḥāt al-arbaʿah

سُبْحَانَ اللهِ

Subḥānal lāh

I declare that Allah is free from imperfections

وَ الْحَمْدُ لِلهِ

Walḥamdu lillāh

And all praise is for Allah

وَ لاَ إِلٰهَ إِلاَّ اللهُ

Wa lā ilāha illal lāh

And there is no god but Allah

وَ اللهُ أَكْبَرُ

Wallahu Akbar

And Allah is greater (than what He is described as)

Perform the *rukūʿ* and the two *sajdahs*
3rd *rakʿah*
1
2
3
4
5
6

- After the 2nd *sajdah* remain seated
- Now recite *tashahhud*
- After *tashahhud* recite the *taslīm*

Tashahhud

اشْهَدُ اَنْ لااِلٰهَ اِلاَّ اللّهُ وَحْدَهُ لاشَرِيكَ لَهُ

Ashhadu a(n)l lā ilāha illa lāhu waḥdahu lā sharīka lah

All praise is for Allah, I testify that there is no god but Allah, He is alone, for whom there is no partner

وَ أَشْهَدُ أَنَّ مُحَمَّداً عَبْدُهُ وَ رَسُولُه

Wa ashhadu anna Muḥammadan ʿabduhu wa rasūluh

And I testify that Muḥammad is His servant and His messenger

اَللّٰهُمَّ صَلِّ عَلىٰ مُحَمَّدٍ وَ آلِ مُحَمَّد

Allahumma Ṣalli ʿalā Muḥammadi(n)w wa āli Muḥammad

O Allah! Bless Muḥammad and the progeny of Muḥammad

Taslīm

اَلسَّلامُ عَلَيْكَ اَيُّها اَلنَّبِيُّ وَ رَحْمَةُ اللّهِ وَ بَرَكاتُه

Assalāmu ʿalayka ayyuhan nabiyyu wa raḥmatullāhi wa barakātuh

Peace be upon you O Prophet, and Allah's mercy and His blessings (be upon you too)

اَلسَّلامُ عَلَينا وَ عَلىٰ عِبادِ اللّهِ الصّالِحِينَ

Assalāmu ʿalaynā wa ʿalā ʿibādillāhiṣ ṣaliḥīn

Peace be upon us and upon the righteous servants of Allah

السَّلامُ عَلَيْكُمْ وَ رَحْمَةُ اللّهِ وَ بَرَكاتُه

Assalāmu ʿalaykum wa raḥmatul lāhi wa barakātuh

Peace be upon you all, and Allah's mercy and His blessings (be upon you too)

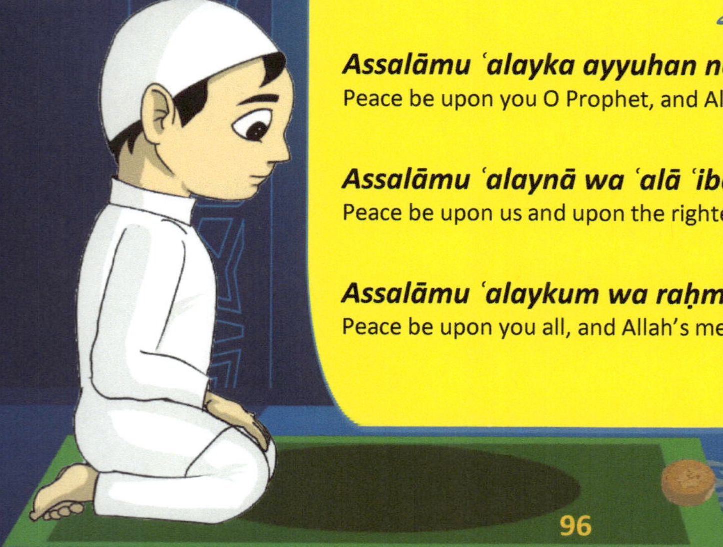

DONE

Now you have completed *Ṣalāt al-Maghrib*. Well done!

After prayers it is recommended to say *dhikr* and *duas*.
Highly recommended to say the *dhikr* of Sayyida Fāṭimah (as).

Dhikr of Sayyida Fāṭimah (as)

اللهُ أكبَر

***Allahu Akbar* x 34**
Allah is greater (than what He is described as)

الْحَمْدُ لِلّهِ

***Alḥamdu lillāh* x 33**
All praise is for Allah

سُبْحانَ اللهِ

***Subḥānal lāh* x 33**
I declare that Allah is free from imperfections

HOW TO PRAY ṢALĀT AL – ʿISHĀʾ

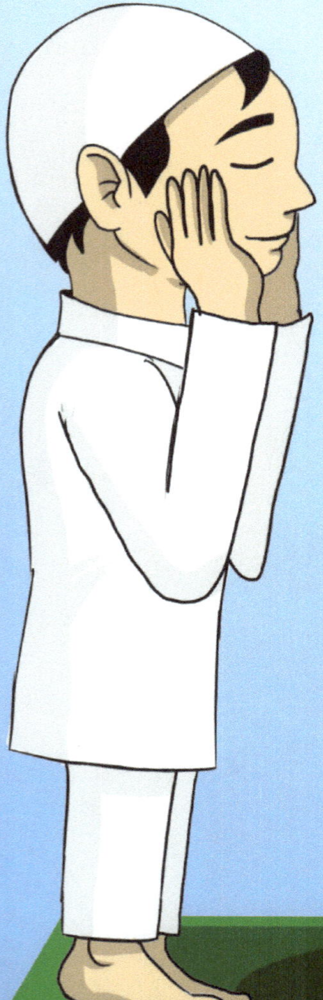

4 x *rakʿahs*

- Perform *Ṣalāt al-ʿIshāʾ* like *Ṣalāt al-Ẓuhr* or *ʿAṣr* except **with the intention of *ʿIshāʾ* prayers** at its prescribed time.

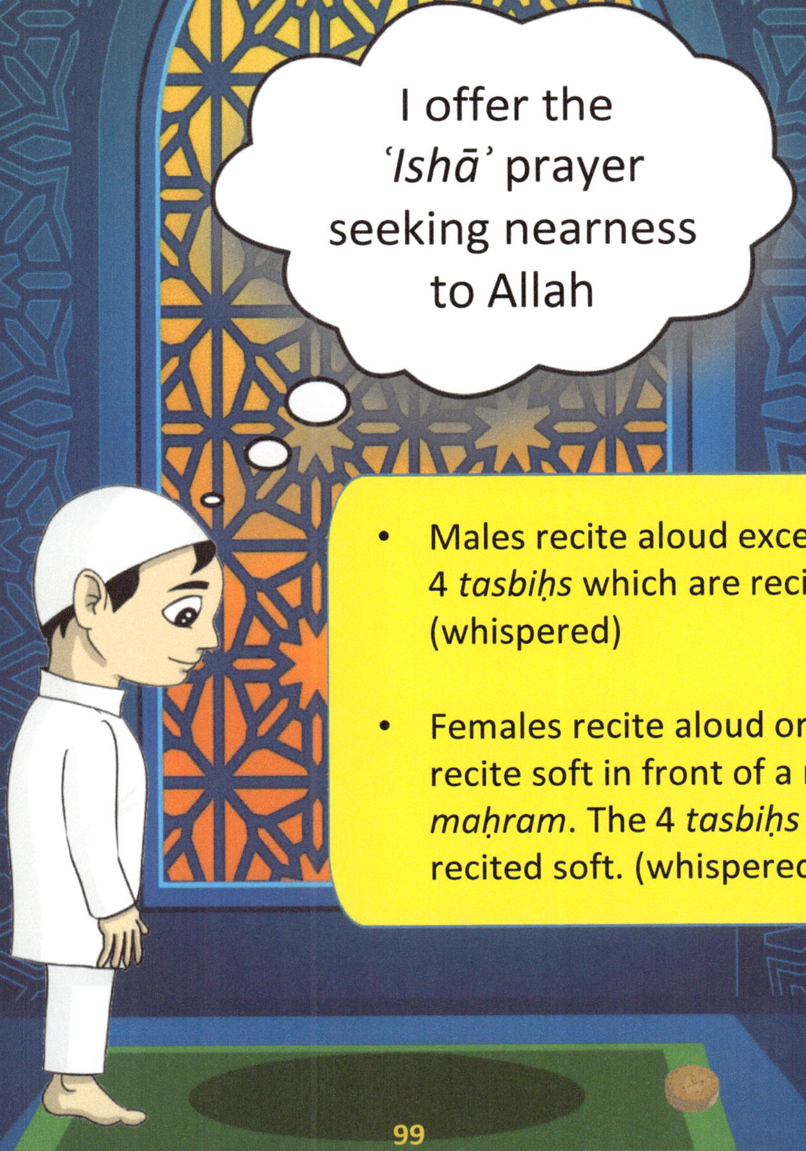

I offer the *ʿIshāʾ* prayer seeking nearness to Allah

- Males recite aloud except for the 4 *tasbiḥs* which are recited soft (whispered)

- Females recite aloud or soft, but recite soft in front of a non-*maḥram*. The 4 *tasbiḥs* are to be recited soft. (whispered)

DONE

Now you have completed *Ṣalāt al-ʿIshāʾ*.
Well done!

After prayers it is recommended to say *dhikr* and *duas*.
Highly recommended to say the *dhikr* of Sayyida Fāṭimah (as).

Dhikr of Sayyida Fāṭimah (as)

اللّهُ أكبَر

***Allahu Akbar* x 34**
Allah is greater (than what He is described as)

الْحَمْدُ لِلّهِ

***Alḥamdu lillāh* x 33**
All praise is for Allah

سُبْحانَ اللّهِ

***Subḥānal lāh* x 33**
I declare that Allah is free from imperfections

WHAT BREAKS MY PRAYER

1. Anything that breaks your *Wuḍūʾ* will also break your prayer, e.g., falling asleep
2. Reciting '*Āmīn*' after Sūrah al-Fātiḥah
3. Turning away from the *Qiblah* (*Kaʿbah* direction) without a legitimate excuse
4. Intentionally saying something apart from what is said during prayer
5. Intentionally laughing out aloud
6. Intentionally crying for worldly things, e.g., crying for a toy, house, car…
7. Eating and drinking
8. Doing something that breaks the form of prayer, e.g., jumping, clapping…
9. Any required pre-condition that is not fulfilled, e.g., *Wuḍūʾ* broken, clothes *Najis*…

For more specifics you can return to our online tutorials or to the original sources

WHAT BREAKS MY PRAYER

Glossary

Dhikr - Remembrance
Dua - Supplication
Ḥarām - Forbidden
Kaʿbah - Sacred Mosque in Mecca
Maḥram - Lit. Forbidden to marry
Makrūh - Not recommended
Mustaḥab - Recommended
Mutlaq - Absolute
Najis - Ritually impure
Non-Maḥram - Lit. Not forbidden to marry
Qunūt - Humility in certain position
Rakʿah - Unit of prayer
Rukūʿ - Bowing
Sajdah - Prostration
Ṣalāt al-ʿAṣr - Afternoon prayer
Ṣalāt al-Fajr - Dawn prayer
Ṣalāt al-ʿIshāʾ - Night prayer
Ṣalāt al-Maghrib - Evening prayer
Ṣalāt al-Ẓuhr - Midday prayer
Sujūd - The act of Prostrating
Sūrah - Chapter
Ṭāhir - Ritually pure
Takbīr - Allahu Akbar
Takbīrat al-iḥrām - The opening *Takbīr*
Tasbiḥ - Glorification
Tasbīḥāt al-arbaʿah - The 4 Glorifications
Tashahhud - Testifying
Taslīm - Salutation
Wājib - Obligatory

Credit

All praise belongs to Allah, the All Merciful towards all existents, the Kindest towards believers. He Who has given us enough patience and courage to complete this book.

Islamic Lessons Made Easy would like to thank all those involved in this project for their hard work and commitment.

EDITORS
Amir Hussein
Kawthar Ibrahim
Sheikh Dr Zaid Alsalami
Sheikh Hossein Javaheri

اللّٰهُمَّ صَلِّ عَلَى مُحَمَّدٍ وَآلِ مُحَمَّدٍ

Allahumma ṣalli ʿala Muḥammadi(n)w wa āli Muḥammad
O Allah, (please do) bless Muḥammad and the Household of Muḥammad

Contact : Admin@islamiclessonsmadeeasy.com.au

Visit us :
Facebook.com/islamiclessonsmadeeasy
Youtube.com/islamiclessonsmadeeasy
Instagram.com/islamic_lessons_me
Islamiclessonsmadeeasy.com.au
Ilme.net.au

ISLAMIC LESSONS MADE EASY

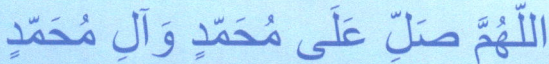

www.ingramcontent.com/pod-product-compliance
Lightning Source LLC
Chambersburg PA
CBHW041102070526
44583CB00002B/33
9781764084208